# Food
# Chemistry

## DAVID E. NEWTON

Facts On File
An imprint of Infobase Publishing

**Food Chemistry**

Facts On File, Inc.
An imprint of Infobase Publishing
132 West 31st Street
New York NY 10001

ISBN-10: 0-8160-5277-8
ISBN-13: 978-0-8160-5277-6

**Library of Congress Cataloging-in-Publication Data**
Newton, David E.
    Food chemistry / David E. Newton.
        p. cm.—(The new chemistry)
    Includes bibliographical references and index.
    ISBN 0-8160-5277-8
    1. Food Industry and trade. 2. Food—Analysis. I. Title
    TP370.N49 2007
    664—dc22      2006033109

Text design by James Scotto-Lavino
Illustrations by George Barile/Accurate Art, Inc.
Project editing by Dorothy Cummings

Printed in the United States of America

MP CGI 10 9 8 7 6 5 4 3 2 1

This book is printed on acid-free paper.

One Last Time . . .
for

John McArdle, Lee Nolet, Richard Olson, David Parr,
David Rowand, Jeff Williams, and John D'Emilio

Thanks for the memories!

# CONTENTS

# PREFACE

The subject matter covered in introductory chemistry classes at the middle and high school levels tends to be fairly traditional and relatively consistent from school to school. Topics that are typically covered in such classes include atomic theory, chemical periodicity, ionic and covalent compounds, equation writing, stoichiometry, and solutions. While these topics are essential for students planning to continue their studies in chemistry or the other sciences and teachers are correct in emphasizing their importance, they usually provide only a limited introduction to the rich and exciting character of research currently being conducted in the field of chemistry. Many students not planning to continue their studies in chemistry or the other sciences may benefit from information about areas of chemistry with immediate impact on their daily lives or of general intellectual interest. Indeed, science majors themselves may also benefit from the study of such subjects.

The New Chemistry is a set of six books intended to provide an overview of some areas of research not typically included in the beginning middle or high school curriculum in chemistry. The six books in the set—*Chemistry of Drugs, Chemistry of New Materials, Forensic Chemistry, Chemistry of the Environment, Food Chemistry,* and *Chemistry of Space*—are designed to provide a broad, general introduction to some fields of chemistry that are less commonly mentioned in standard introductory chemistry courses. They cover topics ranging from the most fundamental fields of chemistry, such as the origins of matter and of the universe, to those with important applications to everyday life, such as the composition of foods and drugs. The set title The New Chemistry has been selected to emphasize the extensive review of recent research and advances in each of the fields of chemistry covered in the set. The books in The New Chemistry set are written for middle school and high school readers. They assume some basic understanding of the principles of chemistry that are generally gained in an introductory middle or high school course in the subject. Every book contains a large amount of material that should be accessible to the interested reader with no more than an introductory understanding of chemistry and a smaller amount of material that may require a more advanced understanding of the subject.

The six books that make up the set are independent of each other. That is, readers may approach all of the books in any sequence whatsoever. To assist the reader in extending his or her understanding of each subject, each book in the set includes a glossary and a list of additional reading sources from both print and Internet sources. Short bibliographic sketches of important figures from each of the six fields are also included in the books.

# INTRODUCTION

F ew topics interest so many different people in so many different ways as does the subject of food. Of course, people need to eat to stay alive, grow and develop, and maintain good health. This need presents ongoing challenges for humans: finding ways of growing crops and raising animals in the most efficient way in the conditions available, inventing methods for competing successfully against plant and animals that also consume the crops and animals on which humans depend, developing methods for preserving foods to make sure they will be available at all times of the year, and so on.

It should be no surprise, then, to discover that a number of chemical techniques used to grow and process foods today have their roots in human cultures of many centuries ago. We tend to think of spices as substances used primarily to enhance the flavor of foods. While they do enhance flavor, many spices were first used as food additives because of their ability to reduce spoilage; their primary purpose was to preserve food. Drying, salting, and smoking are other methods of food preservation still widely used that have origins extending to the earliest years of human existence.

Once a person's basic need for food for survival has been met, foods serve a number of other functions. Meals are often the central event in the life of a family, a neighborhood, or a community, occasions when people can come together to share essential elements in their lives. Those events range from the religious, such as the seder served by Jews during the Passover, to the more secular, such as the Thanksgiving dinner shared in many American homes. The host of cookbooks on every imaginable type of cuisine and food preparation now available attests to the fact that foods are more than simply a means of survival today. They have become as important a part of our culture, at least to some people, as sports, politics, or work.

Food preparation in the 21st century is, of course, more than simply an extension of the methods developed by primitive peoples centuries ago. Indeed, it has become a complex scientific industry that owes as much to the development of modern chemistry as it does to folk traditions and customs. The food industry had its origins in the late 1800s, when chemists began to make discoveries concerning the way in which crops were grown, animals bred and raised, and food processed for human consumption. Chemicals were discovered that added color, flavor, or texture to foods; that retarded decay; that improved the nutritional value of foods; and, in some cases, actually replaced certain *natural foods.*

Over the past two centuries, chemists have continued to push forward the frontiers of food design and development. Today, virtually every technique that is available to the industrial or research chemist is employed by the food chemist to modify the composition of natural foods or even to create new foods with no counterpart in the real world. One of the great challenges for consumers in the 21st century is to learn more about and decide how to use the host of synthetic and semisynthetic foods now available to them.

The involvement of chemists in food modification practices is a double-edged sword. For all the improvements it may have produced in the diet available to humans, the chemical modification of foods has raised many questions about safety and benefits. Are processed foods really equivalent or preferable to natural foods? Are the processes by which food is modified relatively safe, or do they carry significant risks for the consumer? Are there limits to the ways in which food can and should be modified? Questions such as these have become part of the daily dialogue of concerned consumers. They are the focus of this book.

# 1
# THE HISTORY OF
# FOOD MODIFICATION

Food is essential to human survival. It provides the proteins, carbohydrates, fat, fiber, vitamins, and minerals needed to stay alive, grow, and stay healthy. Food also serves other social and religious functions. Seder meals, birthday dinners, awards banquets, wake buffets, and other food-related functions bring people together for a host of cultural purposes. In some fundamental ways, the role of food in human society has probably not changed very much in thousands of years.

People seldom eat foods taken directly from nature—an apple picked from the tree or a raw piece of tuna pulled from the ocean. Instead, they peel, chop, steam, salt, cook, or otherwise modify foods before they eat them. Processed foods have been part of the human diet from the beginning of human culture and still are, but to a much greater extent and in far more sophisticated ways. Food today is still treated by some very old processes, such as salting and drying, but it is also modified in ways resulting in products that barely resemble natural foods. Probably the most important single factor in the way food processing has changed over the past 2,000 years is chemical science. Researchers have found ways of adding chemicals to foods to change their flavor, color, texture, or other properties. They have developed methods for changing the physical and chemical

1

composition of foods to make them more nutritious or palatable. They have even invented new foods that do not exist in nature.

Modern techniques of food modification have both benefits and risks. They make it possible, for example, for people to enjoy foods year round that were once available for only limited times of the year. These techniques enable people in all parts of the world to have nutritious foods that extend their lives and reduce the risk of disease. They present a range of new kinds of foods that earlier generations could hardly have imagined.

But the modified foods produced by chemical research also have their downside. Some new products may contain additives that are harmful to human health. The development of these foods may create hazards for the physical and biological environment. And the development of new foods may be driven by concerns other than people's best interests—by the desire to make an economic profit, for example—that may not justify the effort.

Questions about the value of modified foods arise frequently in today's world. What constitutes a "good" food versus a "bad" food? Are natural foods always and inherently better for people than processed foods? When does the use of chemical substances or chemical technologies improve the value of food, and when are they likely to reduce its nutritional value or create other kinds of problems for the consumer? Consumers often do not know the answers to these questions.

## From Smoked Mastodon to Salt Pork

Questions about the value and safety of different categories of food are especially difficult to answer because people have been modifying foods almost since the dawn of civilization. In fact, without certain types of food modification, the human species might never have survived on Earth.

By far the most common and oldest type of food modification used by humans is food preservation. Imagine, for instance, a community of early humans in northern Europe trying to survive a long, cold winter with no method for preserving food. Or picture a group of hunters in tropical Africa who have just killed a huge animal that could provide them with meals for weeks. In both cases, men and women faced the problem of preserving food that has become available at one time for use at a later time—often, much later.

Over the millennia, people have discovered a variety of methods for keeping food from "going bad"—in other words, decaying. Cooking, smoking, freezing, and drying were among the earliest food preservation techniques. The use of a broad range of spices, the most important of which was salt, also proved effective as a way of preserving foods.

Although early humans developed a variety of methods for preserving food, it is doubtful that they knew anything about the mechanisms by which such techniques preserved foods; they simply knew that they worked. Deeper understanding did not come about until the 19th century, when researchers such as the French chemist Louis Pasteur (1822–95) and the German bacteriologist Robert Koch (1843–1910) discovered the role of microorganisms in the decay of organic material and the spread of disease. These scientists were able to show that certain environmental conditions favored the growth of bacteria (heat and moisture), while others discouraged their survival (cool temperatures and a dry environment).

This information helped explain the success of various food preservation techniques. For example, drying preserves foods because it removes much of the moisture that bacteria need to grow. Freezing works because it lowers the temperature of food to the point that the growth of bacteria is severely inhibited. Spices are effective for a variety of reasons, one being that they may release chemical compounds that are toxic to bacteria; cloves, for example, release a compound called eugenol that slows the growth of bacteria. And smoking food preserves it because smoke, like spices, contains a number of chemicals that inhibit the growth of bacteria. One of the most widely used of modern synthetic preservatives, butylated hydroxyanisole (BHA), is a natural component of smoke.

# Food Additives: Advances and Challenges

Various additives help preserve food, but humans have been adding chemicals to foods for many centuries for reasons other than preservation. Spices have long been used as food additives not only because they may retard the rate of decay but also because they improve the flavor of food that is bland or that has, in fact, already begun to spoil. Additives have also been used to enhance the color of food, reflecting the common belief that people "eat with their eyes" as well as with their palates. Saffron, for example, has long been used to add a bright yellow color to certain types of food, increasing their appeal to the eye as well as augmenting their flavor. Recipes for improving the color of butter with a touch of saffron go back at least to the 14th century.

Adding substances to foods for less than benign reasons—a process known as the adulteration of food—also has a very long history. The adulteration of essential foods, such as bread and wine, extends at least as far back as ancient Egypt. In that society, bakers who sold adulterated bread risked having their ears nailed to their shop doors, a penalty prescribed by law. Many centuries later, the Roman statesman Cato (234–149 B.C.E.) wrote about the problem of watered wine and suggested that a method be developed to discover if winemakers were employing the practice. Two centuries later, another Roman philosopher, Pliny the Elder (23–79 C.E.), described the adulteration of bread with chalk and cattle fodder. Such substitute ingredients were popular among bakers (and other food purveyors) because they were cheaper than genuine ones and increased the profit earned on products sold.

Legislation against food adulteration was haphazard and difficult to enforce until the mid-19th century, primarily because methods for the analysis of foods were primitive and unreliable. Exceptions to that rule occurred. One example was a law enacted by King Edward I (1272–1307) that declared that any baker who had adulterated his product should be dragged through the streets from the Guild Hall to his home with the adulterated bread hanging from his neck. For a second offense, a baker was sentenced to be placed into a pillory; for a third offense, the law required that the baker give up his profession and called for his ovens to be destroyed.

At about the same time, a number of Italian states passed laws designed to discourage the watering and adulteration of wine. And a French law adopted in 1574 forbade the use of food coloring in pastries to simulate the presence of eggs.

One of the earliest campaigns against food adulteration was launched by a German-born English chemist by the name of Friedrich Accum (1768–1838). Accum was concerned about the widespread use of alum, or potassium aluminum sulfate ($KAl(SO_4)_2$), to whiten bread. He analyzed a number of samples of bread available for sale in London and, in 1820, published a book on his findings, *Treatise on Adulterations of Food and Methods of Detecting Them*. The book discussed not only the problems created by using alum in bread, but also a number of other ways in which food processors adulterated their products, usually without the knowledge of the general public.

Other common practices at the time included the addition of sand and sawdust to sugar, the watering of milk, and the addition of salts of iron to beer. As if that were not enough, used tea leaves were dried and re-sold, chilies were added to bran, and coffee was adulterated with chicory. Enraged by Accum's research, which criticized them, millers and bakers joined other food processors and hounded the chemist until he was banished from the United Kingdom and forced to return to his native Germany. This action did not prevent Accum's work from having long-term impact, however: The British parliament, impressed with his findings, passed the nation's first food laws 40 years later, in 1860.

## Food Legislation in the United States

People expressed concern about the adulteration of foods rather early in American history. For example, in 1641, the General Court of Massachusetts passed a law specifying the size and cost of a loaf of bread. Any baker who violated the provisions of the act was required to destroy his or her complete stock of bread. Similar provisions were made to ensure that butter was not being adulterated by dairy workers.

As in England, however, it was not until the mid-19th century that more vigorous efforts to adopt legislation on food adulteration began to appear. In 1862, President Abraham Lincoln appointed the first chemist to the U.S. Department of Agriculture. He was Charles M. Wetherill (1825–71), a student of the great German chemist Justus von Liebig (1803–73). Wetherill began an active program of chemical research, analyzing the chemical composition of foods, fertilizers, pesticides, and other agricultural substances. His first project focused on the use of grapes for wine making. One question he asked was whether the addition of sugar during the wine-making process could be thought of as adulterating the wine. He decided that it could not. When the Food and Drug Administration decided 46 years later that sugar *was* to be considered an adulterant in wines, it only highlighted the difficulties in making such decisions.

Toward the end of the 19th century, two major trends in the United States emphasized the need for federal control over the manufacture, processing, and distribution of foods and drugs. First, the way Americans obtained their food began to change dramatically. Second, remedies known as patent medicines hit the markets.

In rural 19th-century America, most families either grew and raised their own food or they purchased it from a nearby source. As the nation became more industrialized, that pattern changed. Farms, ranches, and dairies became increasingly mechanized and industrialized. They transported their produce to large cities, perhaps hundreds of miles away, where they were sold days, weeks, or even months later. This system not only required a much greater use of food preservatives but also encouraged the development of new kinds of foods: Foods with "improved" flavor, color, ease of preparation, and other qualities were designed to appeal to increasingly sophisticated and busy urban consumers. Many of the issues that Accum had raised in Great Britain in the 1820s began to reappear in the new American system of food preparation, distribution, and sale. In some common methods of food adulteration practiced at the time, dairies thickened cream with additives (often, calf's brains), sellers added mineral oils to salad oils, cheap cider was converted to "red wine" with the addition of lead coloring, boric acid was added to sponge cakes, dust and arsenic were added to cocoa, and sand was added to brown rice and brown sugar to increase their bulk.

The late 1800s also saw the introduction and rapid growth of a patent medicine industry in the United States. Patent medicines are nonprescription drugs that are usually protected by a trademark and whose ingredients are not disclosed to the general public. By 1900, newspapers and magazines were filled with ads for products such as Kick-a-poo Indian Sagwa, Warner's Safe Cure for Diabetes, Hamlin's Wizard Oil, Godfrey's Patent Chloride of Ammonium Inhaler, Dr. Sheldon's Magnetic Linamint, Mother Graves Worm Exterminator, and Dr. Williams Pink Pills for Pale People. Manufacturers of these products promised relief from virtually every disease and disorder known to humans. A product known as Vitadatio, for example, promised to relieve consumption, kidney troubles, bladder troubles, diabetes,

Dr. Guertin's Nerve Syrup is an example of the patent medicines that became popular in the late 1800s with promises of curing a broad range of diseases and disorders. (National Library of Medicine)

◄ **HARVEY WASHINGTON WILEY (1844–1930)** ►

Convincing legislators to pass the nation's first food and drug laws required extraordinary efforts from many concerned and informed individuals. Near the top of that list was Dr. Harvey W. Wiley, Chief Chemist of the U.S. Department of Agriculture from 1882 to 1907 and the first Chief Administrator of the Food and Drug Administration from 1907 until 1912.

Wiley was born in a log farmhouse near Kent, Indiana, in 1844. He earned his bachelor's degree from Hanover College in 1867 and his M.D. from Indiana Medical College in 1871. He then briefly attended Harvard College, which awarded him a second bachelor's degree in 1873. Wiley then returned to Indiana in 1874 where he became a professor of chemistry at the newly created Purdue University and taught chemistry, physics, and other sciences. One of Wiley's major fields of interest at Purdue was food adulteration. He studied sugar chemistry and attempted to analyze sugars and syrups to discover whether and how they had been adulterated.

Wiley was apparently considered for the post of president at Purdue on three different occasions, in 1875, 1883, and 1900. Trustees opted not to offer him the position on the first occasion because he was a bachelor and they considered him to be too young and too undignified. He was widely known, for example, to have turned a blind eye to the restless enthusiasm of the college students whom he supervised. Indeed, so popular was he among students that the school's 1908 yearbook declared him "Father of Purdue Athletics." By 1883 and 1900, Wiley had become too involved in his work in Washington to consider returning to Purdue.

piles, cancer, insomnia, nervous debility, epilepsy, ringworm, sciatica, poverty of blood, wasting disease, indigestion, gall, Bright's disease, stricture, rheumatism, gout, eczema, and all other diseases of the blood and skin. Users of the product were promised that they would "get cured of the leprosies of malignancy, and . . . by virtue of renewed vigour, enjoy life in a rational reasonable manner." Patent medicines were, however, almost entirely without any demonstrated medical benefit except for the pain-relieving and euphoric effects produced by the opium, morphine, heroin, cocaine, and/or alcohol that was often their active ingredient.

Wiley was appointed Chief Chemist of the U.S. Department of Agriculture in 1882. He arrived in Washington with considerable experience in the testing of foods for adulterants. (He later wrote a fundamental textbook on the subject, *Foods and Their Adulterations,* published in 1907 and revised in 1911.) Wiley realized that the country needed tough laws that would prevent food processes from adulterating food with chemicals that could cause illness and death among consumers.

One of Wiley's most dramatic programs to demonstrate this principle was his so-called Poison Squad, launched in 1902. The Poison Squad consisted of 12 volunteers who agreed to subsist on a diet that might—or might not—include potentially poisonous food additives. Wiley designed his scientific study carefully, measuring changes in the volunteers' height, weight, temperature, pulse rate, and other physical traits, attempting to determine the effect of their having eaten foods laced with additives. The study went awry, however, as news of the Poison Squad's activities were leaked to the press. Soon, newspaper readers throughout the nation had learned of Wiley's experiment. Wiley ended the research when his volunteers became seriously ill because of the additives they had been ingesting. By that time, however, public opinion and the minds of legislators were focused on the problem to which he was trying to call attention and, within a few years, the Pure Food and Drug Act of 1906 was passed.

Wiley died in Washington in 1930 and was buried in Arlington Cemetery.

Public concern about the new food-processing systems and the plague of patent medicines eventually led to the passage of the Pure Food and Drug Act of 1906. It was the first federal legislation in the United States dealing with foods and drugs. The act had three major outcomes. First, it created the Food and Drug Administration (FDA) and made it responsible for evaluating all foods and drugs intended for human use in the United States. Second, it defined a category of drugs that could be sold only by prescription. Finally, it required manufacturers to list ingredients of any potentially addictive drug or medicine (such as the patent medicines) on the product's label.

The Pure Food and Drug Act of 1906 had some valuable immediate effects: It dramatically reduced the manufacture and sale of patent medicines. But it had relatively little effect on the changing methods and systems by which food was produced, processed, and distributed. Food sellers continued to develop ways to modify natural foods to increase their sensory appeal, to improve their health benefits, to increase their shelf lives, and to make them more attractive in other ways to consumers. Indeed, these trends continue to the present day and food chemists still constantly look for new ways to manipulate foods to increase their market appeal.

For all its weaknesses, the Pure Food and Drug Act has remained the cornerstone of U.S. regulations on food safety for more than a century. The U.S. Congress made a number of changes and additions to the act on a few occasions, most notably the Federal Food, Drug, and Cosmetics Act (FDCA) of 1938, which extended and expanded the 1906 legislation and specifically prohibited interstate commerce in adulterated food.

By the mid-20th century, yet another change in the food industry began to emerge: the manufacture of synthetic foods, products that contain few or no natural foods of any kind. Anyone who has read food labels carefully has encountered such foods. For example, what food product contains the following list of ingredients: corn syrup solids, vegetable oil (partially hydrogenated coconut or palm kernel, canola, hydrogenated palm, soybean, cottonseed, or safflower), sodium caseinate, dipotassium phosphate, mono- and digylcerides, artificial flavor, and annatto color? (The food product is non-dairy creamer.)

None of this discussion is to suggest that all methods of food processing are undesirable. Indeed, food-processing techniques have made significant strides to increase the nutritional value of foods, as well as to make them more appealing to consumers. Perhaps more importantly, food additives have been used to prevent and control a variety of nutritional disorders.

An example is the disorder formerly known as goiter. In the mid-1920s, Dr. David N. Marine, Sr., and his colleagues in Michigan, Ohio, and West Virginia studied this condition. Symptoms include a swelling at the base of the neck, which can become as large as a grapefruit, mental retardation, low IQ, deafness and/or mutism, stunted physical growth, and reduced resistance to disease—conditions that can, in extreme cases, lead to death. Pregnant women who develop goiter are likely to miscarry.

Marine and his colleague found that the addition of small amounts of iodine to a person's diet reduced the risk of the disorder essentially to zero. Goiter today is more commonly referred to as iodine deficiency disorder, or IDD. IDD develops when a person's diet lacks an adequate amount of the mineral iodine.

As a result of his studies, Marine became convinced that "[s]imple goiter is the easiest of all known diseases to prevent. . . . It may be excluded from the list of human diseases as soon as society determines to make the effort." Iodine, used as a food additive, could prevent the illness. By 1924, people in many parts of the United States could purchase "iodized salt," ordinary table salt (sodium chloride; NaCl), to which had been added a small amount of potassium iodide (KI). Within two decades, the percentage of American households using iodized salt had reached 75.8 percent, and IDD had largely been eradicated in the United States. That percentage has remained essentially the same since the 1950s in the United States. By contrast, IDD remains a serious health problem in many parts of the world where availability of iodized salt is limited.

Iodine is only one of many vitamins and minerals now added routinely to foods in the United States. The vitamins thiamine (vitamin $B_1$), riboflavin (vitamin $B_2$), and niacin (another B vitamin) are added to flour, breakfast cereals, rice, cornmeal, and egg products; vitamin A is added to a number of dairy products, such as skimmed and evaporated milk, milk products, and margarine; iron is added to infant formulas, meat and meat products, egg products, and foods designed for people with special nutritional needs; and zinc is added to breakfast cereals, egg products, infant formulas, and plant-based beverages.

The Pure Food and Drug Act of 1906 laid the legislative and regulatory groundwork for the monitoring of foods in the United States. The act made some important strides in protecting the American public from the worst excesses of food adulteration. At the same time, food chemists continued to develop new products for the food

## ◄  PAUL KARRER (1889–1971)  ►

One of the greatest developments in food modification technology during the 20th century was the synthesis of vitamins, which could then be added to foods. A major figure in this work was the Swiss chemist Paul Karrer. Karrer was born in Moscow on April 21, 1889, of Swiss parents living in Russia at the time. He attended the University of Zürich, from which he obtained a Ph.D. in 1911. After a brief period spent at the Georg Speyer Haus at Frankfurt am Main, he returned to Zürich, where he took a post as professor of chemistry. In 1919, he was also appointed director of the Chemical Institute.

Karrer's early research involved a study of the carotenoids, the yellowish-orange compounds responsible for the color of carrots, tomatoes, egg yolk, sweet potatoes, and other foods. He identified and found the chemical structure for a number of different carotenoids. By the early 1930s, however, he had turned his attention to the vitamins.

Vitamin deficiency diseases, such as rickets, beri-beri, and pellagra, had ravaged human populations since the dawn of civilization. Such diseases can be avoided if one eats a diet that includes all the necessary vitamins and minerals. Many people in many parts of the world do not have access to such diets. A simple way to combat vitamin-related nutritional problems, however, is simply to add vitamins to food that is available.

industry. Some of these products, such as nutritional additives, significantly improved the quality of food available in the nation. Other advances in food chemistry, however, had less beneficial effects on food quality.

## Advances and Issues in Food Laws and Legislation

Because it was the first federal piece of legislation dealing with food safety, the Pure Food and Drug Act of 1906 was an important milestone in protecting consumers from unsafe foods and drugs. But that act had a number of serious shortcomings. For example, the law was unclear as to what constituted a safe food or drug. Courts found

The problem was that chemists knew almost nothing about the existence or chemical structure of vitamins. Then, in a flurry of activity, that problem yielded to the efforts of a handful of researchers, including Karrer, from a variety of countries. Once these structures were known, chemists were able to begin the process of finding ways to synthesize them so that they could be mass produced as food additives.

In 1931, Karrer announced the correct structural formula for vitamin A, a compound that is closely related to the carotenoids. This discovery was the first case in which a complete and correct structural formula for a vitamin had been determined. Proof of his results came when Karrer and his colleagues first made the vitamin synthetically in the laboratory, the first time a vitamin had been produced artificially.

Karrer went on to determine the formula of and to synthesize a number of other vitamins, including riboflavin (vitamin $B_2$) in 1935 and vitamin E (tocopherol) in 1938. During his lifetime, Karrer published more than 1,000 scientific papers dealing with vitamins, carotenoids, and other organic compounds. In recognition of his work with vitamins, Karrer was awarded a share of the 1937 Nobel Prize in chemistry. He remained at the University of Zürich until his retirement in 1959. Karrer died in Zürich on June 18, 1971.

it difficult to convict food adulterators because they had no specific guidelines of "food purity" to follow. In addition, a food processor or drug manufacturer could be convicted only if it had intentionally produced a product with the purpose of harming people; it fell to the government to prove intent.

Defects in the 1906 act became increasingly apparent also as food and drug scientists continued to make advances. Their discoveries and inventions, such as the production of new kinds of food additives, were quickly incorporated into processed foods and new drug formulations. The regulations of 1906 soon became outdated: As science and technology made rapid steps forward in the two decades after adoption of the 1906 act, governmental interest in and regulation of foods and drugs changed not at all.

By the 1930s, public advocates were once again demanding that the government take a more active role in food and drug regulation. Manufacturers of such products, of course, warned against government interference in people's right to make choices about the products they purchase. Food producers, processors, distributors, and retailers feared the government regulation would reduce profits.

As is often the case, it took a terrible tragedy to change the regulatory climate. In 1937, a small drug manufacturer, S. E. Massengill Company, released on the market a new "miracle drug," sulfanilamide, in a liquid formulation they called Elixir of Sulfanilamide. Not unreasonably, Massengill believed that many patients would prefer to take the new drug as a liquid rather than in pill form or by having an injection. For some reason, however, the company used diethylene glycol as the solvent. Diethylene glycol is very toxic, and in the first few months that the new product was on the market, 107 people died as a result of taking it. The public soon learned that Massengill could not be prosecuted for selling a toxic product, although it was fined $16,800 for having a false label on the bottles in which it was sold.

The Massengill disaster energized legislators, and by the following June Congress had enacted and President Franklin D. Roosevelt had signed the Federal Food, Drug and Cosmetic Act of 1938. This act had several improvements over its 1906 predecessor. First, it required drug manufacturers to test new products before marketing them and to submit scientific evidence for these tests to the federal government. In addition, it prohibited the addition of poisonous substances to food. (This regulation had not existed before!) The act also established specific standards for the production and processing of foods and authorized programs of factory inspections. Finally, it set more stringent penalties for anyone who violated the new laws.

The history of food modification legislation in the United States (and other countries of the world) has largely consisted of efforts by governmental agencies to keep up with new advances in food science and technology. The government is usually at a disadvantage in this contest since regulators may not even be aware of new breakthroughs in food science and technology until they have actually reached the marketplace.

This pattern is clear in the series of federal laws that were adopted in the decades after the 1938 act. In the years following World War II, for example, the federal government continually tried to write new regulations that would deal with the rapid scientific advances that had come about as a result of war-related research and other developments in food science and technology. Between 1954 and 1960, three major amendments to the 1938 act were adopted. The first of these was the 1954 Pesticide Amendment, which dealt with the types of chemical products that could be used on agricultural crops destined for the marketplace. The next was the 1958 Food Additives Amendment, which, for the first time, provided strict definitions as to what constituted an "additive" and prescribed how additives were to be tested before use. Most important, it included a section known as the Delaney Clause, which severely restricted additives that had been shown to cause cancer in experimental animals. Finally, the 1964 Color Additive Amendment focused on the increasingly popular use of chemicals to alter the color of foods sold to consumers.

The most recent set of governmental regulations dealing with foods and drugs was the FDA Modernization Act of 1997, which attempted to bring the FDA up to date with changes that had been made in food and drug technology in the four decades since the 1954–60 amendments. The 1997 act addressed a wide variety of problems, ranging from the need to modernize systems used by the FDA to test and certify foods and drugs, to the issue of changes in labeling policies for foods and drugs, to the adoption of new policies and practices for regulation of medical devices and for new medical products.

The race between food scientists trying to develop new products for the marketplace and government regulators trying to ensure that such products are safe and effective shows no sign of stopping. Indeed, at the dawn of the 21st century, a number of new questions have arisen about food safety and a number of old questions have once again come to the forefront. Food scientists have made enormous strides in the manufacture of genetically engineered foods, products that do not exist in the natural world (although their close cousins may), and these foods might play a major role in the human diet of the not-so-distant future. Also, nutrition experts and consumers are asking once more about claims being made for so-called natural, whole, and organic foods. Advances such as these are likely to continue to raise issues for the general public and for regulators of food safety.

# 2
# FOOD ADDITIVES

The U.S. Food and Drug Administration (FDA) maintains a data-base called "Everything" Added to Food in the United States (EAFUS); available at http://vm.cfsan.fda.gov/~dms/eafus.html. This database contains the names of more than 3,000 substances that are, have been, or may be legally added to foods in the United States. A number of the items listed in the EAFUS are compounds, elements, and mixtures familiar to students in a beginning chemistry class, such as acetic acid, aluminum hydroxide, benzene, calcium chloride, cloves, cobalt sulfate, glucose, iron, magnesium sulfate, ozone, phenol, phosphoric acid, sodium chloride, sulfuric acid, and vitamin A. But the EAFUS also contains a number of substances that would probably be unfamiliar to most chemistry students, substances such as astaxanthin, 2-benzofurancarboxal-dehyde, cadinene, beta-caryophyllene, dragon's blood extract, and E-2-(2-octenyl)cyclopentanone.

The EAFUS database contains up to 196 distinct pieces of information on each item listed in it. The use and safety of every substance is categorized into one of five classes, ranging from safe and widely used, to used but of uncertain safety, to unsafe and, therefore, banned from use as a food additive. The compound 4-propyl-2,6-dimethoxyphenol, for example, is grouped as "NIL," meaning that there are toxicological data about the compound but also there is no report of its being used as a food additive. The compound cobalt sulfate, by contrast, is in the class called "BAN," indicating that it has been banned from use as a food additive because of toxicological information about its dangers to human health. Compounds in this category (BAN) were, however, used at one time or another as food additives.

The EAFUS database provides an indication of how large and complex the field of food additives has become. It also shows how many foods contain products whose chemical properties are still not understood.

The use of food additives today still reflects to some extent the way they have been used in the past. But the very large number of food additives recorded in the EAFUS list also is an indication of the vast variety of ways in which these substances are applied today. These applications can be categorized into three major groups: preservation, improvements in nutritional value, and enhancement of marketability.

# Preservation

Foods spoil due to two primary causes: the action of microorganisms living in the food and the natural decay processes that take place in food itself. In each of these cases, chemical changes that take place in the food are responsible for spoilage.

Microorganisms such as bacteria, yeasts, and mold occur naturally in all foods. They grow and reproduce using the nutrients found in food to carry out their own metabolism. When these metabolic processes release noxious and/or toxic by-products, the result is spoilage. By-products of microbial metabolism have various effects on the taste, appearance, and healthfulness of foods. Some "spoiled" foods, such as sauerkraut or kim chee, have tastes that some people find offensive but others enjoy. The real danger of spoiled foods is the toxic products that they eventually contain, posing health threats to humans who eat them.

## PRESERVATION FROM MICROORGANISMS

As noted in chapter 1, one set of techniques for the preservation of food is designed to kill microorganisms, to reduce or stop their growth, or to prevent them from reproducing. The methods used are generally either physical or chemical.

Physical methods of food preservation are designed to alter the environment in which microorganisms live, making it difficult or impossible for them to survive. Most microorganisms have certain common requirements for their survival: the presence of oxygen (for aerobic microorganisms), moisture, heat, and a certain optimal level of acidity. Physical methods of food preservation deprive microorganisms of one or more of these conditions. For example, heating food to some minimum temperature (pasteurization) can kill the microorganisms present in the food, preventing the food from spoiling or reducing the rate of spoilage. Freezing is less effective as a method of food preservation than pasteurization because it does not necessarily kill microorganisms, although it greatly reduces their rate of metabolism. Drying can be an effective method of food preservation because it deprives microorganisms of the moisture they need to live and reproduce. As with all methods of food preservation, each physical technique is more effective with some types of food and less effective with others. One of the most promising forms of food sterilization is radiation, discussed in chapter 5.

Chemical methods of food preservation act directly on microorganisms by altering their biochemical structure or the biochemical reactions used in their metabolism and reproduction. Chemical methods can be divided into three major categories:

1.  methods that change the permeability of a microorganism's cell membrane, preventing it from obtaining the nutrients it needs for its survival and thus causing its death;

2.  methods that interfere with a microorganism's biochemical reactions, usually involving the disruption of a specific *enzyme* activity and thus causing the microorganism's death; and

3.  methods that block or interfere with the biochemical reactions involved in reproduction, preventing the growth of new microorganisms.

A key factor in many of these methods is *pH*. pH is a measure of the acidity of a solution and is equal to the negative logarithm of the hydrogen ion concentration of the solution, or:

$$pH = -\log [H^+].$$

The pH scale ranges from 0 to 14, with low pH numbers representing acidic solutions and high pH numbers representing alkaline solutions. The pH of pure water and any neutral solution is 7.0.

Scientists have determined that relatively few microorganisms can survive at a pH of less than 4.6, and for many of the most virulent microorganisms, the optimal pH is much higher. The table shows the optimal pH range for the survival of some common bacteria.

Organic and inorganic acids that retard or prevent spoilage by lowering the pH of food are some of the most widely used chemical preservatives. In many cases, these acids also interrupt one or more of the microorganism's biochemical reactions. Such compounds are sometimes known as *microbial antagonists* because their molecular structure is sufficiently similar to a second molecule to allow it to compete for positions on a microbe's chemical receptors. Some ex-

◁ **OPTIMAL pH FOR VARIOUS TYPES OF MICROORGANISMS** ▷

| MICROORGANISM | pH |
|---|---|
| Bacteria | about 7.0 |
|    E. coli | 6.0–8.0 |
|    Salmonella | 6.8–7.5 |
|    Streptococci | 6.0–7.5 |
|    Staphylococci | 6.8–7.5 |
|    Clostridium | 6.0–7.5 |
| Fungi | about 5.6 |
| Protozoa | 6.7–7.7 |
| Algae | 4.0–8.5 |

amples of microbial antagonists currently in wide use are benzoic acid, sorbic acid, propionic acid, paraben, compounds of sulfur, and nitrates.

Benzoic acid ($C_6H_5COOH$) and its salts, the benzoates, are found naturally, most commonly in cranberries, prunes, and cinnamon. In addition to lowering the pH of food, benzoic acid and the benzoates interfere with the action of microbial enzymes that catalyze oxidative phosphorylation; that is, they prevent the microorganisms from storing the energy released when it metabolizes food. They also bind to and inhibit substances in the microorganism's cell membrane, reducing its ability to transport essential substances into the cell interior. Benzoic acid is most effective against molds, somewhat less effective against yeasts, and differentially effective against bacteria. It is used most commonly for the preservation of fruit juices, syrups, soft drinks, relishes, and margarine. The substance is usually used in the form of one of its salts, such as sodium or ammonium.

Sorbic acid ($CH_3CH = CHCH = CHCOOH$) and the sorbates reduce the pH of food, react with chemicals in the cell membrane to reduce membrane transport, and interfere with a variety of enzymes involved in the cell's metabolism, especially the enolase and dehydrogenase enzymes. The foods to which sorbic acid is most frequently added are dairy products, primarily cheeses, meats, baked goods, prepared salads, pies and cakes, and pickled products. It is usually added in the form of calcium or potassium sorbate.

An interesting by-product of the use of benzoates and sorbates as food additives was announced in 2000. Scientists at the University of Rochester Medical Center discovered that these compounds may reduce the rate of tooth decay. Rats fed a diet of fluorides and benzoates or sorbates had fewer cavities than those whose diets contained fluorides only. The discovery was a happy surprise because these additives are so widely used today that everyone gets the benefits they provide—apparently including fewer cavities—without making any special effort.

Propionic acid ($CH_3CH_2COOH$) occurs naturally in certain fruits, such as apples and strawberries, and in tea and violets. When added to foods, it binds to molecules on the surface of microorganism cell membranes, reducing and stopping the flow of materials into and out of the cell. Inside the cell, it reduces pH, interfering with the organism's ability to metabolize normally. It acts most effectively against molds but can be used against certain types of spore-forming bacteria called rope-formers. Propionic acid and the propionates are used in baked goods, cheeses, and dairy products. It is usually added to foods in the form of its calcium or sodium salts, calcium or sodium propionate.

The term *paraben* refers to any of the alkyl esters of para-hydroxybenzoic acid. These compounds are especially effective in preventing the growth of molds and yeasts. Some of the esters that have been used as food additives are methylparaben, ethylparaben, propylparaben, butylparaben, and heptylparaben. Heptylparaben finds some limited use as a preservative in malt beverages and soft drinks where it appears to inhibit the growth of spores in bacteria such as *Bacillus* and *Clostridium*. The most common preservative formulation consists of a mixture of methyl and propyl esters. Such formulations are used in baked goods, jams and jellies, soft drinks, certain dairy products, and some kinds of fish and meat. Chemical structures for two paraben preservatives are shown below.

Compounds of sulfur called sulfites act both as microbial antagonists and as antioxidants, substances that prevent or retard the natural decay of foods. In the first role, they block the action of

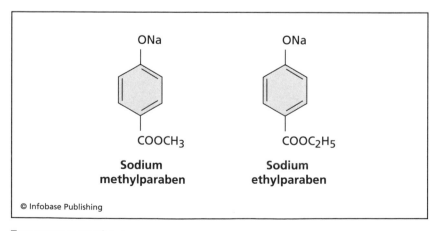

© Infobase Publishing

Two common parabens

two enzymes critical to the formation of ATP (adenosine triphosphate), the "fuel" living cells use to produce energy. When these two enzymes, glyceraldehyde-3-phosphate dehydrogenase and alcohol dehydrogenase, are inhibited, the microorganism cell is unable to generate ATP, and it dies. Sulfites inhibit these two enzymes by disrupting both the sulfur bonds in cysteine, one of the amino acids present in their molecular structure, and the disulfide bonds that hold the enzymes in their three-dimensional structure. This structure is what allows them to bond to food molecules, so when it has been destroyed, the enzymes are unable to continue functioning.

In common usage in the food industry, the term *sulfite* refers to a group of related chemical species that includes sulfur dioxide ($SO_2$), sulfurous acid ($H_2SO_3$), the sulfite ion ($SO_3^{2-}$), and the bisulfite ion ($HSO_3^-$). The form in which sulfur occurs depends on various factors, the most important of which is pH. At low pH, the acid form ($H_2SO_3$) predominates and is most active.

Sulfur and its compounds are among the oldest chemical preservatives known. There is some evidence that the ancient Egyptians used such compounds to sterilize their wine barrels, and the burning of sulfur among the Romans for the purpose of sterilization is well documented. According to the Food Additives and Ingredients Association, sulfites are the most widely used of all food preservatives today. Large amounts are used as preservatives in the production of wine and vinegar. Probably their most important use is in the treatment of fruits and vegetables that have just been harvested, to protect the products against attack by molds and yeasts.

Nitrates ($NO_3^-$) and nitrites ($NO_2^-$) are used primarily to cure meats. One function is to retain the red color that most people regard as a sign of meat that is fresh and healthful. The red color is produced by a series of reactions that occur when a nitrate or nitrite (such as potassium nitrate [$KNO_3$] or sodium nitrite [$NaNO_2$]) has been added to meat. When the additive is a nitrate, the first step in that process is the reduction of the nitrate to the nitrite:

$$NaNO_3 \rightarrow NaNO_2$$

Microorganisms that occur naturally in meats, such as *Micrococcus*, catalyze this reaction. In the next step, the nitrite is converted to nitrous acid, which is then further reduced to nitric oxide (NO):

$$NaNO_2 \rightarrow HNO_2 \rightarrow NO$$

In the final step of this process, the nitric oxide reacts with myoglobin in meat, converting it to nitrosomyoglobin, a compound with a bright red color characteristic of fresh meat.

Nitrates and nitrites play a second critical role as additives to meat and meat products: They inhibit the production and germination of *Clostridium botulinum* spores. This bacterium is the organism responsible for the deadly disease known as botulism, one of the most virulent diseases known to humans.

The agent thought to inhibit *C. botulinum* is nitrous acid, which oxidizes amino ($NH_2-$) groups readily. Nitrous acid reacts with and deaminates cytosine, converting it to uracil (see the figure below). Since cytosine is a component of all DNA molecules, this reaction radically alters those molecules, converting them into a form that does not permit normal replication and transcription. This action of nitrous acid is thus thought to be responsible for the deactivation and inhibition of essential enzymes used by the *C. botulinum* bacterium, especially the dehydrogenases and oxidases.

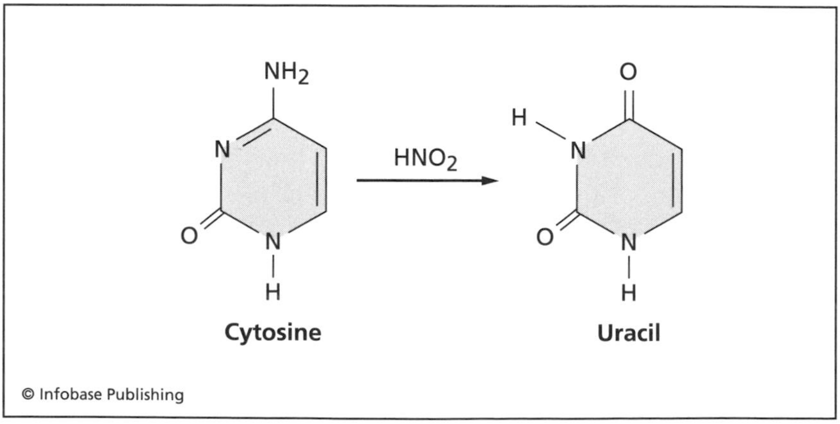

© Infobase Publishing

Conversion of cytosine to uracil by nitrous acid

A fairly recent addition to the tools used for food preservation is the *modified atmosphere packing (MAP)* concept. Researchers have learned that they can extend the shelf life of many foods by selecting appropriate packaging materials and the appropriate atmosphere in which to store them. This concept is hardly new. It dates to at least 1795 when the French confectioner Nicolas (François) Appert (ca. 1750–1841) discovered vacuum packing of food. Without actually understanding the scientific principles involved, Appert found that storing foods in a can void of air retards the rate at which they spoil. Today it is understood that vacuum packing deprives microorganisms of the oxygen they need to grow and reproduce, reducing the rate at which toxins are released into the stored food.

Some forms of MAP employ Appert's original design. Food is placed into a gas-impermeable bag, from which air is almost totally removed (vacuum packaging) or partially removed (low-pressure or hypobaric packaging). In either case, microbial action is reduced because of the low levels of oxygen available for their growth and reproduction.

In another form of modified atmospheric packaging, food is stored in a gas-impermeable bag to which is added a specific mixture of oxygen, nitrogen, and/or carbon dioxide. Mixtures high in oxygen concentration (*high-oxygen MAP*) are used almost exclusively for the storage of meats. Such mixtures usually contain about 70 percent oxygen, 20–30 percent carbon dioxide, and 0–10 percent nitrogen. The high concentration of oxygen inside the package ensures that sufficient amounts of the gas will be available to combine with myoglobin in the meat, producing its characteristic "fresh" red color. Packaging containing mixtures low in oxygen and high in nitrogen and/or carbon dioxide is similar in some ways to vacuum and hypobaric packaging. Reduced levels of oxygen retard the rate of microbial growth, extending shelf life of the product. In addition, carbon dioxide gas itself may also act as a microbial antagonist in at least two different ways. First, carbon dioxide dissolves in water to form the weak acid carbonic acid ($H_2CO_3$). Carbonic acid ionizes to form hydrogen, bicarbonate ($HCO_3^-$), and carbonate ions ($CO_3^{2-}$), lowering the pH of the food:

$$CO_2 + H_2O \rightarrow H_2CO_3 \rightarrow H^+ + HCO_3^- \rightarrow H^+ + CO_3^{2-}$$

### ◁ NICOLAS (FRANÇOIS) APPERT (ca. 1750–1841) ▷

It is easy for people living in the 21st century to take food preservation for granted. Almost anywhere in the world, a person can walk into some kind of store and purchase foods that have been preserved by canning, bottling, freezing, drying, or some other method. In the early 1800s, however, most of the techniques that are widely available today had not yet been invented. The first such technique to have been developed was canning, a process discovered by the French cook and confectioner Nicolas (François) Appert.

Appert was born in Châlons-sur-Marne, France, about 1850 (1749 per some sources, 1752 per others). His father was an innkeeper, and young Nicolas (also known as François) received extensive on-the-job training as a cook in his early years. Like many in his position, he became interested in the problem of preserving foods and decided to experiment on different methods for preventing spoiling. Coincidentally, the French government had become very much interested in the same problem at about the same time. In 1795, Napoléon Bonaparte had announced a 12,000 franc prize for anyone who could develop a method of food preservation, and Appert accepted the challenge. He worked for 14 years on a variety of methods until he found a system that worked. The system he developed was sub-

As pH is lowered, the rate of bacterial survival, growth, and reproduction declines. Second, all forms of carbon dioxide (the gas itself, carbonic acid, and the ions it produces) are thought to interfere with essential biochemical reactions carried out by microbial cells. Evidence suggests that these species may affect the permeability of microbial cell membranes, interfere with the action of certain amino acids in cells, and inhibit the action of certain enzymes involved in cell metabolism.

All of the modified atmospheric packaging systems just described make use of a passive packaging material, usually a chemically inert plastic, and depend on the gases injected into the package for their food preservation action. Another recently developed approach involves the use of an "active" or "intelligent" packaging material. Here the material itself contains one or more substances that are gradu-

mitted to the Consulting Bureau of Arts and Manufacturing for testing and found to be successful. In 1809 he was awarded the 12,000-franc prize and wrote *The Art of Preserving all Kinds of Animal and Vegetable Substances for Several Years,* a pamphlet describing the system that was published in 1811.

At the time, virtually no experiments had been conducted on the methods by which food spoils, so Appert had no theoretical background for his studies. He simply tried one method after another until he discovered one that protected food from spoilage. The system consisted of immersing glass bottles in boiling water, injecting the food into the bottles, and then sealing the bottles with a cork top, wire, and sealing wax. When carried out correctly, the system protected foods from spoilage for months and even years.

Appert's work was widely acknowledged in his native country. In 1812, he was awarded a gold medal by the Society for the Encouragement of National Industry, and a decade later, he was given the title "Benefactor of Humanity." He also founded a commercial cannery that survived until 1933. Appert was not himself, however, as successful. His success had been tied closely to that of Napoléon, and with the emperor's downfall, Appert's star also went into decline. Most of his factories were destroyed in Napoléon's overthrow, and Appert himself died in poverty in Massy, near Paris, on June 3, 1841.

ally released into the package and reduce the rate of spoilage of the food.

In an *active packaging system,* some antimicrobial substance is incorporated into the packaging material itself during production. In one series of experiments, for example, sorbic acid and potassium sorbate were added to the wax used to wrap cheese, where the compounds helped to destroy molds that cause cheese to spoil. The additive is usually formulated such that it will be released from the wrapping material slowly over time. In some cases, it is designed to adhere permanently to the inner surface of the packaging material. When a food is wrapped in the treated packaging, the antimicrobial agent slowly migrates out of the wrapping material and diffuses throughout the food, where it performs its preservative function. In addition to antimicrobial actions, active packaging systems may perform as oxygen scavengers (to reduce the rate of natural food decay), moisture scavengers (to reduce the concentration of moisture inside the package), and ethylene scavengers (to remove a gas released during the ripening of fruit).

Active packaging technology is less than two decades old, and many questions have yet to be answered, for instance: What antimicrobial agents can be used and what wrapping materials are most suitable for their deposition? What are the best methods for depositing an agent into a given wrapping material? Under what conditions are the agents best able to act on the foods? Thus far, researchers have tried a number of antimicrobial agent–wrapping combinations in a variety of physical formats. For example, some traditional organic acids (sorbic, benzoic, and propionic) have been implanted into polyethylene wrapping, carbon dioxide gas into cellulose wrapping, and propionic acid into ionomer-polymer wrapping. One of the most interesting lines of research focuses on attempts to implant microbial agents into edible types of wrapping. For example, in one experiment, sorbates were injected into an edible biopolymer for use in food packaging. The challenge with this line of research, of course, is to find antimicrobial–wrapping combinations that are not only effective in reducing spoilage but also safe for human consumption.

Thanks to developments in the food sciences over the past century, food processors now have a number of chemicals available to them as food additives for protection against spoilage as a result of the action of microorganisms. In addition, researchers continue to explore new methods of food preservation, such as modified atmospheric packaging, which holds promise for revolutionizing methods by which foods are preserved.

## PRESERVATION FROM NATURAL DECAY

Another form of spoilage occurs when food begins to break down by natural processes of decay. This process takes place when enzymes naturally present in foods interact with (usually) oxygen and/or water, breaking down the food's carbohydrates, *lipids,* proteins, and other biochemical compounds into their component parts. This type of spoilage has a number of manifestations.

One such change is *rancidity*. When a fat or oil decomposes into its fundamental components, fatty acids and glycerol, it is said to have become rancid. Fats and oils, members of the chemical family of lipids, are esters of the trihydric alcohol known as glycerol ($C_3H_5(OH)_3$) and long saturated and/or unsaturated fatty acids that have the general formula $CH_3(CH_2)_nCOOH$, where $n$ is of the order of 10, 12, 14, 16, or 18. The equation below shows the general changes that take place when an enzyme oxidizes or hydrolyzes (reacts with water) a lipid to form glycerol and fatty acids.

The fatty acids produced by such reactions typically have unpleasant odors that make some types of food inedible. For example, when butter begins to spoil it develops an "off" smell caused by the presence of butyric and other organic acids. These organic acids form when the fatty acid esters that make up butter begin to hydrolyze and oxidize.

The oxidative and hydrolytic reactions by which fats and oils are converted to glycerol and fatty acids are complex, and are catalyzed by inorganic catalysts (metal ions), enzymes (lipoxidases) that occur naturally in food, and forms of energy, such as sunlight. In all cases,

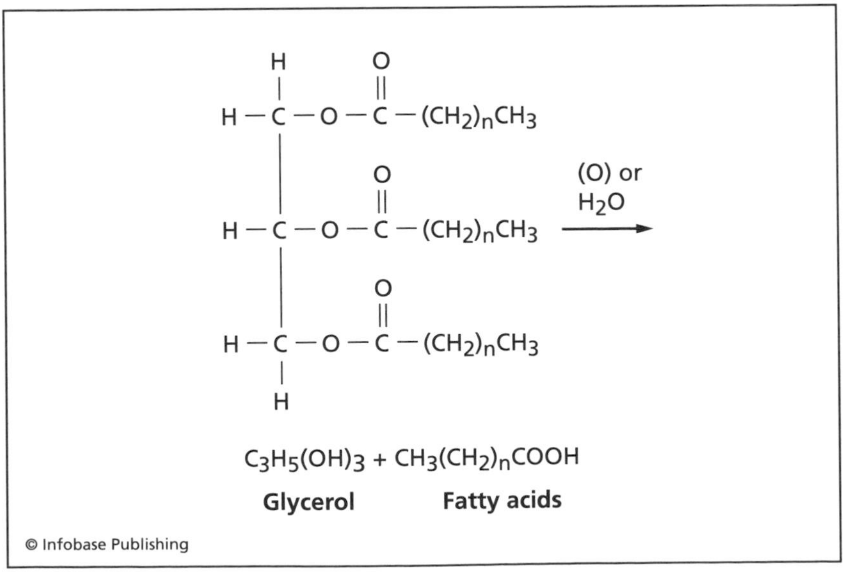

© Infobase Publishing

Oxidation or hydrolysis of a lipid

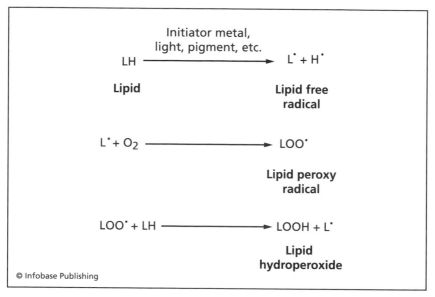

Auto-oxidation of lipids

the catalysts cause lipid free radicals to form at the double bonds in a lipid molecule. A lipid *free radical* is a portion of a lipid molecule containing a single, unpaired electron. These highly reactive structures react readily with free oxygen molecules, forming other free radicals known as lipid peroxy radicals. Lipid peroxy radicals then react with other lipid molecules to form lipid hydroperoxides (the primary products of oxidative rancidity) and additional lipid free radicals. The process is, thus, self-perpetuating once it has been initiated. The sequence of events in this auto-oxidative process is outlined above.

To prevent the decomposition of fats and oils, then, chemists must find substances that (1) react with lipid free radicals and/or (2) react with oxygen. Either reaction will arrest the auto-oxidative process just described. A rather large number of substances have been found that meet either or both of these criteria. The chemical structures of some of the most common of these substances are shown in the diagram on page 31. In the past, probably the most widely used of these free radical scavengers were BHA and BHT, used best in combination. More recently the use of naturally occurring substances, such as ascorbic acid (vitamin C) or one of the tocopherols (vitamin E), has gained favor wherever it is possible.

Another natural change that unfavorably affects the appearance, odor, and flavor of food is *browning*. This term refers to the process that occurs when the surface of fruits, vegetables, and shellfish has been cut or bruised. Most people have observed this reaction in their

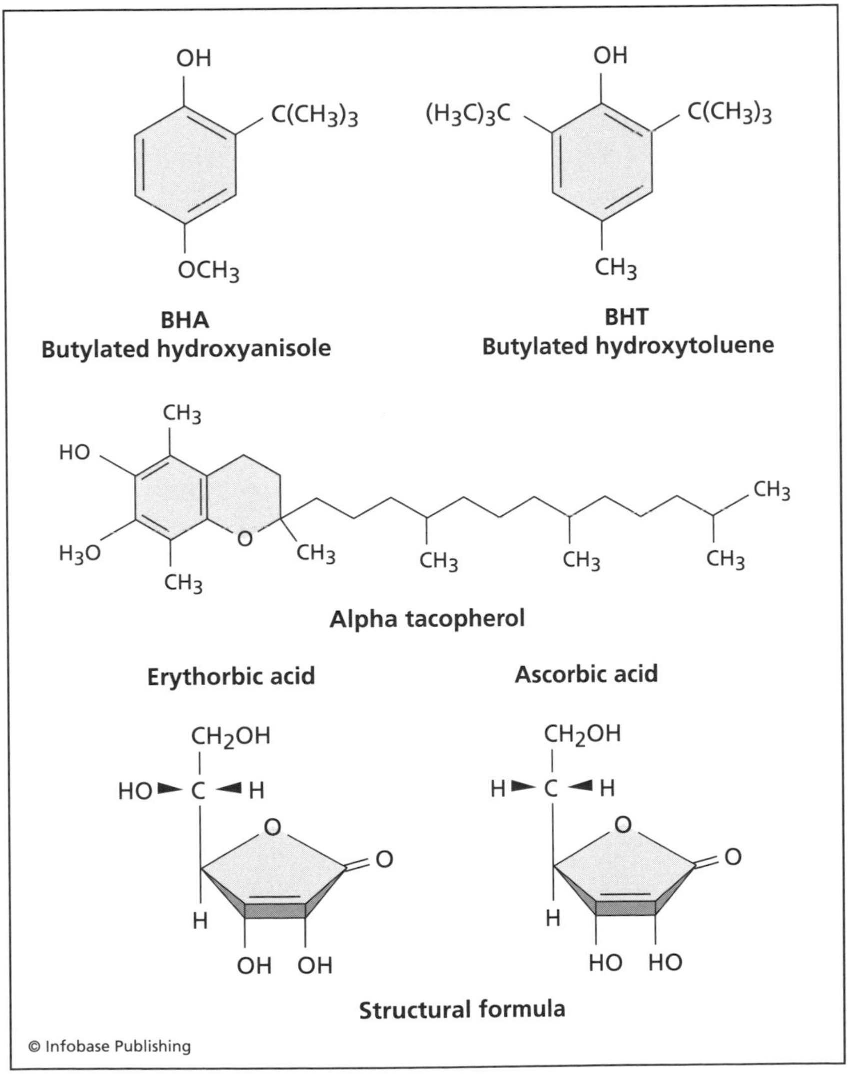
OH
C(CH3)3
OCH3
BHA
Butylated hydroxyanisole
OH
(H3C)3C
C(CH3)3
CH3
BHT
Butylated hydroxytoluene
CH3
HO
H3O
O
CH3
CH3
CH3
CH3
CH3
CH3
Alpha tacopherol
Erythorbic acid
CH2OH
HO C H
O
O
H
OH OH
Ascorbic acid
CH2OH
H C H
O
O
H
HO HO
Structural formula
© Infobase Publishing

Chemical structures of some common free radical scavengers

own kitchen. An apple, potato, or banana that has been sliced gradually begins to turn brown and, within half an hour, no longer looks good enough to eat. The two known forms of browning are enzymatic and nonenzymatic (or Maillard) browning.

Enzymatic browning occurs when enzymes that occur naturally in plant materials react with phenolic compounds in the fruit or vegetable. The enzymes most commonly involved are the polyphenol oxidases, or PPOs. PPOs are copper-containing proteins that react readily with phenol-based constituents of plant foods such as tyrosine and catechol. They catalyze two reactions: The first converts the phenol to a diphenol (as shown below) and the second converts the diphenol to a quinone. The quinones thus formed then begin to polymerize, forming a brownish pigment responsible for the discoloration of bruised or cut fruits and vegetables.

One of the most effective additives for the prevention of browning is sulfite. Sulfite reacts with quinone to prevent polymerization,

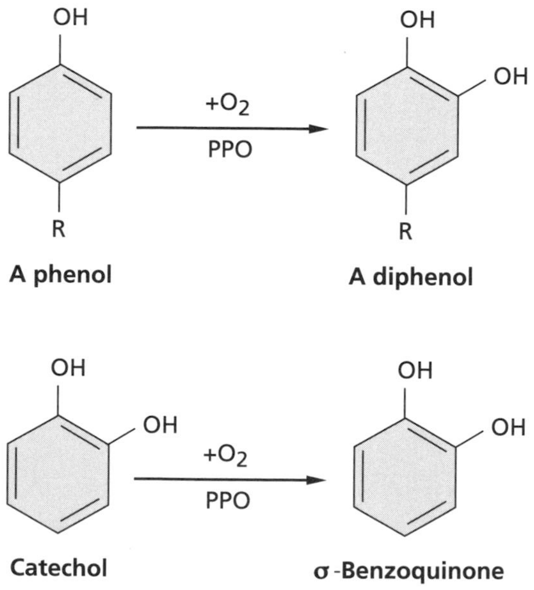

OH                          OH
                              OH
    +O₂
    PPO

R                           R
A phenol                    A diphenol


OH                          OH
    OH                          OH
    +O₂
    PPO

Catechol                    o-Benzoquinone

© Infobase Publishing

Enzymatic browning

and hence, it prevents a brown color from developing. Other additives have been found to effectively inhibit the polymerization of quinone, among them ascorbic acid, citric acid, 4-hexylresorcinol (4HR), and ethylenediamine tetraacetic acid (EDTA).

Nonenzymatic browning occurs when sugars and proteins in foods begin to react with each other. The process is quite complex, involving about two dozen steps (the Maillard reaction). It is initiated when the carbonyl group ($>C=O$) of a sugar reacts with the amino group of a protein or amino acid, splitting out water and forming a compound known as a N-glycosylamine. The process ends with the formation of another brownish-colored polymer, melanoidin. In the early stages of the reaction, the chemical products give the food a light brown color and a sweet smell, characteristic of the caramelization process. As the reaction proceeds, the color becomes darker and the odors less pleasant.

Nonenzymatic browning occurs ubiquitously, in both raw and cooked foods. The reactions by which browning develops are strongly affected by heat, and many common cooking and baking techniques encourage their development. For example, the odors and colors that develop when sugar is caramelized, when bread is baked, and when fruits and vegetables are stored for long periods are all caused by Maillard reactions.

Sulfites are very effective in reducing nonenzymatic browning. They combine with and inactivate sugars that would otherwise react with amino groups, halting the Maillard reaction at its outset. As a secondary effect, they act as bleaching agents; they remove the brown coloring that might otherwise be developed as a result of Maillard reactions. Today sulfites are essentially the only additives being used to deter nonenzymatic browning.

Food preservation has long been a part of human culture. Without methods of preservation, people would be limited to eating only fresh foods at the times of the year when they are available. More important, people would be subject to a number of food-borne diseases that develop in spoiled foods. Food chemists have developed a host of chemicals that can be used in the preservation of foods. These preservatives extend the variety of foods available and provide protection against disease caused by spoiled foods.

Critics sometimes object to the use of so many chemicals in food preservation, claiming that such chemicals may cause allergic reactions, cancer, or other health conditions. The goal of a responsible program of food preservation is to conserve the values offered by preservatives without introducing new risks to human health from the preservatives themselves.

## Nutritional Enhancement

Arguably the most significant change that has taken place in the health of Americans over the last century is the dramatic decrease in the occurrence of nutritional disorders. These disorders result from insufficient intake of one or more dietary nutrients. They include the major vitamin-deficiency diseases of pellagra (insufficient amounts of niacin in the diet), scurvy (lack of vitamin C), rickets (lack of vitamin D), beriberi (lack of thiamine), and pernicious anemia (lack of vitamin $B_{12}$) as well as mineral-deficiency disorders such as anemia (deficiency of iron) and goiter (deficiency of iodine).

During the early decades of the 20th century, nutritional deficiency diseases were major causes of illness and death in the United States and elsewhere. First observed in the United States in 1902, pellagra spread rapidly throughout the nation, especially in the South. Nationwide, an estimated 3 million cases and 100,000 deaths attributable to the disease were reported in the next four decades. The pattern for rickets was similar. In 1921, rickets was considered the most common nutritional disease of children in the United States. It was said to affect about three-quarters of all infants in New York City.

The idea that people's diets must include trace amounts of certain substances (vitamins and minerals) to protect against diseases such as scurvy, rickets, and beriberi evolved over the course of two centuries. That process began in the mid-18th century with the discovery by Scottish physician James Lind (1716–94) of the presence of an "antiscurvy factor" in limes. By the early 20th century, a handful of these nutritional "factors" had been discovered. In 1912, the Polish-American biochemist Casimir Funk (1884–1967) suggested the name of *vitamine* (the final *e* was later dropped) for the organic members of this group.

Once the existence of these essential compounds and their crucial role in maintaining human health had been recognized, researchers began to determine their chemical structure and to synthesize them in the laboratory. The first breakthrough in this effort came in 1934 when the English chemist Sir Walter Haworth (1883–1950) discovered the chemical structure of vitamin C (ascorbic acid) and synthesized the compound in his laboratory. For the first time in history, it was possible to produce one of those essential trace elements that protected humans against a nutritional disease, scurvy.

Over the next decade, chemists discovered the chemical structures of four other vitamins, permitting their synthesis in the laboratory: vitamins A and $B_2$ (riboflavin) in 1935, $B_1$ (thiamin) in 1936, and E in 1938. These discoveries made possible a revolution in the food-processing industry. For the first time, it became possible to add chemicals to foods that would protect people against a host of terrible diseases. By 1938, producers of flours and breads were being encouraged to add thiamin, niacin, riboflavin, and iron to their products to protect consumers against a variety of nutritional deficiency disorders. Five years later, those recommendations became mandatory requirements of the Food and Drug Administration. As these recommendations and requirements were put into force, the rate of pellagra, scurvy, rickets, beriberi, and anemia began to plummet. Today, most practicing physicians have never seen a case of any one of these disorders.

Vitamins and minerals are added to foods for one of two reasons: restoration or *fortification*. Restoration is the process of returning to foods vitamins and minerals that are lost during the process of production. For example, during the process of milling, up to half of the original vitamins and minerals in flour may be lost, largely as a result of the removal of wheat germ. *Enriched* flour is flour to which equivalent amounts of those vitamins and minerals have been restored.

Fortification is the process of adding vitamins and minerals to foods that otherwise do not contain them or that normally contain them but at lower concentrations. The addition of potassium iodide to salt, of iron to bread, and of calcium to orange juice are examples of fortification in which vitamins and minerals are added to foods

## ◄ WALTER NORMAN HAWORTH (1883–1950) ►

People sometimes worry about the addition of "chemicals" to our foods by food corporations. Yet one class of food additives, the vitamins and minerals, have probably done more to improve the general health of Americans than any other product used by the food industry. This step only became possible, however, when chemists in the early 20th century began to analyze naturally occurring vitamins and determine their structures, making it possible for them to be synthesized in the laboratory. With the discovery of synthetic methods for making the vitamins, they could soon be produced abundantly at low cost, making them available for widespread use as food additives.

An important figure in this process was the English chemist Walter Haworth. Haworth was born on March 19, 1883, in Chorley, Lancashire, in the northwestern part of England. Haworth left school at the age of 14 to work in his father's linoleum factory, where he became intrigued about the use of dyes in the manufacture of linoleum. He became convinced that he was more interested in the chemistry of dyes than he was in managing a linoleum factory, and he began to take private lessons to prepare for the university. With this training, Haworth was able to pass the entrance exam to Manchester University in 1903, where he studied under William

in which they do not naturally occur. One reason for this practice is to increase the likelihood that consumers will get the nutrients they need from a larger variety of foods. Another reason is that it allows food manufacturers to promote the health value of such foods to consumers.

Today, in fact, many foods are "over-fortified," in the sense that they contain larger amounts of vitamins and minerals than might actually be necessary from a nutritional standpoint. For example, some forms of breakfast cereals claim that they provide 100 percent of the vitamins and minerals a person needs in his or her daily diet. That claim may then be used to justify a considerably higher price for the cereal than one might pay for an unfortified breakfast cereal. The problem is, of course, that a person gets vitamins and minerals from a number of foods in the daily diet

Perkin, Jr., son of the discoverer of synthetic mauve. In 1906, he received his degree in chemistry from Manchester and was awarded a scholarship to the University of Göttingen, where he earned his doctorate in one year. He then returned to Manchester as Perkin's assistant and, four years later, was awarded a second doctorate by Manchester.

Haworth taught briefly at the Imperial College of Science and Technology in London and then, in 1912, took a position at United College at the University of St. Andrew's in Scotland, where he organized a program for the production of chemicals needed in the war effort of World War I. After the war, he took a position at Armstrong College in the University of Durham, where he remained until 1925. In that year, he moved to the University of Birmingham, where he did most of his research on the structure of vitamin C. In 1934, he announced that he had determined the chemical structure of the vitamin, a relatively simple molecule containing six carbon atoms, six oxygen atoms, and eight hydrogen atoms, centered on a five-membered ring containing one oxygen atom and a double bond. In recognition of this accomplishment, Haworth was awarded a share of the 1937 Nobel Prize in chemistry. He was knighted in 1947.

During World War II, Haworth again focused his efforts on the war effort, devoting his work to the production of purified uranium for use in fission bombs. He died unexpectedly on March 19, 1950, in Birmingham.

and does not (or should not) rely on getting all of those nutrients from a single source, whether a breakfast cereal or some other food.

In spite of the risk of over-fortification, the nutritional enhancement of foods has been one of the great accomplishments of food chemistry in the past century. Today Americans have virtually no concern about developing deficiency diseases such as scurvy and rickets because their foods contain all the nutrients they require to be protected from such conditions.

## Enhancement of Marketability

Eating is not an automatic, boring routine that people go through in order to stay alive. Indeed, for most people, meals are pleasurable experiences in which diners savor the color, flavor, odor, texture, and other properties of the foods they eat. Corporations that prepare foods for sale have always been aware of this fact, and they have developed hundreds of food additives that enhance the attractiveness of food to consumers. The food additives used to increase the marketability of foods usually do little or nothing to make food safer, more healthful, or more long-lasting. They just make it more enjoyable to consume.

Some of the earliest food additives people used were naturally occurring substances that enhance the color, odor, or flavor of food. Historians know of dozens of natural substances used over the centuries to enhance the physical appeal of foods. The list includes rose petals to provide a reddish color to food, indigo stone for blue tints, saffron to add yellow, spinach juice to produce a greenish tint, violet flowers to give a purple color, and finely ground gold or silver to provide a metallic tint.

It was not until the latter 19th century, however, that chemists began to synthesize products that could be used as artificial food additives for the enhancement of color, odor, and flavor. The first such breakthrough was the discovery by Sir William Perkin (1838–1907) in 1868 of the structure of coumarin, a benzene derivative with the pleasant odor of new-mown hay. Perkin began to market coumarin as the first synthetic perfume, marking the beginning of the artificial perfume industry. In addition to its pleasant odor, coumarin has a flavor very similar to that of vanilla, and for many years it was popular as the first synthetic food flavoring, replacing the far more expensive natural vanilla bean. Coumarin retained its popularity until the mid-1920s, when its toxic effects on the liver and kidneys were discovered. By that time, however, a research team consisting of the German chemist Ferdinand Tiemann (1848–99) and the French chemist Wilhelm Haarmann (1847–1931) had discovered the chemical structure of vanillin, the compound that gives vanilla its odor and taste. They began to manufacture vanillin as an artificial substitute for the natural product.

One major breakthrough in the early history of flavor chemistry was the discovery of the properties of the alkyl esters of organic acids, that is, compounds formed when an alcohol (such as methyl alcohol) reacts with an organic acid (such as butyric acid). This class of compounds has flavors and odors remarkably similar to a number of natural products. The first of these esters, methyl anthranilate, is said to have been discovered accidentally by German chemists searching for new perfumes. The *ester* filled the room with an overwhelming smell of grapes, making the product ideal as a flavor additive for foods. The ester is still the component primarily responsible for the flavor of grape Kool-Aid.

Today, flavor chemists have developed an extensive list of alkyl esters that can be used as artificial flavors. Some of these compounds actually occur in the plants that they smell like, while others do not. The chart on page 40 lists some of the synthetic flavors most commonly used today.

In spite of the pronounced odors of the alkyl esters, the most popular food additives used for flavoring are aldehydes. They are, in order of the amount used in foods annually: ethyl vanillin and vanillin (3-methoxy-4-hydroxybenzaldehyde; vanilla flavor), cinnamaldehyde (cinnamon flavor), and benzaldehyde (cherry flavor).

Today, the FDA authorizes the use of nine synthetic compounds and 21 naturally occurring substances for use as color additives in foods. These substances are listed in the chart on pages 41–42.

The FDA has also certified about 150 naturally occurring substances and more than 800 synthetic chemicals for use as flavor additives. The chart on page 43 lists a few examples of each of the approved groups.

Clearly, many additives are available to impart specific flavors and appealing colors to foods. In addition to these, food processors now add a number of other substances, some natural and others, mostly synthetic substances, to enhance other physical properties, extend shelf life, and make foods easier for consumers to work with. Some examples of those additives are the following: acidulants and alkalies, bleaching agents, emulsifiers, firming agents, humectants, leavening agents, stabilizers, surface active agents, and thickeners.

Acidulants and alkalies are added to foods to increase or decrease their acidity or "tartness." Examples of products used to increase acidity and tartness are acetic acid, citric acid, lactic acids, sorbic acid, and tartaric acid. Compounds used to decrease or counteract

◁ **SOME ALKYL ESTERS WITH**
   **DISTINCTIVE FLAVORS** ▷

| NAME OF ESTER | FLAVOR |
| --- | --- |
| methyl butyrate | apple |
| ethyl butyrate | pineapple |
| amyl acetate | banana |
| isoamyl acetate | pear |
| amyl butyrate | apricot |
| octyl acetate | orange |
| ethylmethylphenyl glycidate | strawberry |
| ethyl anthranilate | Concord grape |
| isobutyl formate | raspberry |
| ethyl formate | rum |
| methyl salicylate | wintergreen |
| methylphenyl acetate | jasmine |

acidity include sodium carbonate, calcium carbonate, and ammonium bicarbonate.

Anticaking agents are designed, as their name suggests, to prevent foods from clumping together. One of the most important applications of anticaking agents is in the salt industry, where sodium

◁ **PERMITTED NATURAL AND SYNTHETIC FOOD COLORING AGENTS** ▷

| NATURAL COLORING AGENTS | SYNTHETIC COLORING AGENTS* |
|---|---|
| annatto extract | FD&C Blue No. 1 |
| beta-apo-8'-carotenal | FD&C Blue No. 2 |
| beta-carotene | FD&C Green No. 3 |
| beet powder | FD&C Red No. 3 |
| canthaxanthin | FD&C Red No. 40 |
| caramel color | FD&C Yellow No. 5 |
| carrot oil | FD&C Yellow No. 6 |
| cochineal extract | Orange B |
| cottonseed flour | Citrus Red No. 2 |
| ferrous gluconate | |
| fruit juice | |
| methylphenyl acetate | |
| grape color extract | |
| grape skin extract | |
| paprika | |

*(continues)*

◄ **PERMITTED NATURAL AND SYNTHETIC FOOD COLORING AGENTS** *(continued)* ►

| NATURAL COLORING AGENTS | SYNTHETIC COLORING AGENTS* |
|---|---|
| paprika oleoresin | |
| riboflavin | |
| saffron | |
| titanium dioxide | |
| turmeric | |
| turmeric oleoresin | |
| vegetable juice | |

*Colors approved according to the Food, Drug, and Cosmetics Act are referred to by designations known as FD&C color numbers.

silicoaluminate is widely used to prevent salt from caking together during transportation and storage. Other popular anticaking agents include calcium silicate and iron ammonium citrate.

Bleaching agents, such as chlorine, chlorine dioxide, and benzoyl peroxide, are used to increase the whiteness of a food product. They are used extensively to bleach flour and other wheat products.

Emulsifiers are used to form suspensions of watery foods with oily foods, such as the oil and vinegar that make up a salad dressing. They are widely used in the baking industry to control the size and texture of breads, cakes, and other products; to improve softness; to increase the volume of products; and to increase shelf life. Some

◁ **SOME EXAMPLES OF APPROVED FLAVOR ADDITIVES** ▷

| NATURAL SUBSTANCES | SYNTHETIC SUBSTANCES |
| --- | --- |
| aloe | benzyl butyrate |
| blackberry bark | cinnamyl propionate |
| buchu leaves | cyclohexyl isovalerate |
| castor oil | diethyl sebacate |
| cubeb | ethyl pyruvate |
| hyacinth flowers | geranyl formate |
| mimosa flowers | isoamyl nonanoate |
| orris root | methyl cinnamate |
| quebracho bark | phenethyl anthranilate |
| rhubarb root | sorbitan monostearate |
| spruce needles | undecyl alcohol |

Source: Adapted from *Code of Federal Regulations,* Title 21, Chapter I, Part 172. Available online. URL: http://lula.law.cornell.edu/cfr/cfr.php?title=21&type=part&value=172.

common emulsifying agents are the polysorbates, sorbitan monostearate, glyceryl monostearate, and the acetic, lactic, citric, and fatty acid esters of glycerol.

Firming agents are substances that, as their name suggests, help foods to maintain a crisp or firm structure. They are often used as additives with fruits and vegetables that tend to grow soft after they have been harvested. They are also added to products like jams and jellies that are expected to retain a firm shape and not become watery or soupy. The most common firming agents are salts of calcium, such as calcium bisulfite, calcium citrate, calcium phosphate, calcium sulfate, and calcium gluconate.

Humectants are substances added to foods to promote the retention of moisture. These additives have the ability to form weak chemical bonds with water, keeping a product from drying out or becoming powdery. Some widely used humectants are propylene glycol, sorbitol, mannitol, glycerine, xylitol, propylene glycol, and polydextrose.

Leavening agents are substances that undergo a chemical reaction that produces carbon dioxide gas. As the gas forms and is warmed, it forms tiny bubbles that cause a product to "rise" and become fluffy. At one time, yeast was the most popular leavening agent used, but its action is not always dependable; it varies based on the age of the yeast culture, the temperature, the food to which it is added, and other factors. Today, the most popular leavening agents are salts of weak acids that hydrolyze (react with water) to produce hydrogen ions. They include sodium bicarbonate (baking soda), sodium aluminum sulfate, calcium biphosphate, aluminum sulfate, and aluminum phosphate.

Stabilizers are added to foods to hold them together and help them maintain a distinctive physical form. In many cases, a stabilizer plays the role of an emulsifier, maintaining a uniform dispersion of two immiscible (unmixable) substances. Some compounds used commercially as stabilizers are calcium carbonate, bicarbonate, and acetate; sodium and potassium citrate; sodium tartrate; and tannins.

Surface active agents are compounds that alter the surface properties of liquid or semisolid foods, so as to produce a variety of effects. For example, they might be used to make a product foamy or to reduce its tendency to foam. They might also be used to prevent a sticky food, such as peanut butter, from sticking to the container in which it is sold. Some common surface active agents are sodium and calcium stearoyl-2-lactylate, petroleum and other forms of wax, and the polysorbates.

Thickeners are used to increase the viscosity (resistance to flow) of food. They are added to salad dressings, cheese spreads, sauces, ice creams, frozen fruits, and other liquid and semisolid foods to produce some desired consistency. A number of natural gums, such as guar gum, gum arabic, and gum tragacanth, are especially popular as thickeners. Various forms of starch used as thickeners include mono- and distarch phosphate and hydroxypropyl starch. Some synthetic compounds used for this purpose are the glycerol mono- and distearates, sodium and calcium stearoyl-2-lactylates, and polyglycerol monostearate (PGM).

Consumers in many parts of the world today have access to a huge variety of foods made possible by the use of food additives that enhance their color, flavor, taste, and other physical properties. Food chemists continue to look for new ways to make foods more interesting and more appealing to consumers in the future. One can safely predict that grocery stores of the mid-21st century will carry an even wider variety of products developed by ongoing research on food additives.

# Regulation of Food Additives

As described in chapter 1, food additives are regulated in the United States on the basis of a series of laws described in chapter 1 including the Pure Food Law of 1906, the federal Food, Drug, and Cosmetic Act of 1938, the 1958 Food Additives Amendment, the 1960 Color Additive Amendment, and the Food Quality Protection Act of 1996. This framework of laws divides food additives into four major categories: generally recognized as safe (GRAS) substances, prior-sanctioned substances, color additives, and other food additives.

The GRAS category was created by the 1958 Food Additives Amendment to simplify the U.S. Food and Drug Administration's effort to ensure that only safe substances were being added to the nation's food. It directed the FDA to prepare a list of additives that it had good reason to believe were safe for human consumption (the

GRAS list). Items on the list would be permitted for use *unless* new data indicated that a substance was *not* safe for human consumption. The FDA published the first GRAS list in the Federal Register in 1958. It contained nearly 200 substances including not only such common additives as salt, pepper, sugar, vinegar, and baking soda, but also a large number of products generally thought to be safe "when used in accordance with 'good manufacturing practice.'" Some items that were placed on the GRAS list originally have since been removed because later data showed that the substance posed a threat to human health. However, more than 2,000 items remain on the FDA's GRAS list today.

The category known as prior-sanctioned substances was also created by the 1958 act, and it included all food additives that the FDA had specifically approved for use prior to passage of the act. This category includes a large number of relatively well-known inorganic chemicals, such as calcium phosphate, oleate, acetate, and stearate; magnesium stearate and phosphate; potassium oleate and stearate; and sodium pyrophosphate and stearate. Probably the most important items in this category from a commercial standpoint are the nitrites of sodium and potassium, which are widely used as preservatives for meats.

The 1960 Color Additive Amendment established special provisions to regulate color additives. It specified substances that could be used as color additives without any further testing or research (those exempt from certification) and additives that were subject to testing and research (those subject to certification).

The fourth category of food additives includes chemicals about which little or nothing is known concerning their effects on human health. Suppose, for example, that a company has discovered or invented a substance that may be useful as a food additive but has never been tested for possible lethal or other harmful effects on human health. In order to obtain FDA permission to use the substance as a food additive, the company must follow a very specific program of testing. The steps in that process are as follows:

1. The FDA reviews chemical information about the proposed new food additive.

2. The FDA conducts studies to determine the probable human exposure to the chemical, should it be used as a food additive. From these studies, the FDA calculates an estimated daily intake (EDI) based on the highest probable use of the food additive.

3. The company submitting the application conducts studies of the effects of the proposed food additive on experimental animals. It finds out how many animals (if any) are killed by the chemical and how many (if any) develop health effects, such as cancer. Guidelines for this research are included in an FDA publication called *Toxicological Principles for the Safety of Food Ingredients*, commonly known as "The Redbook."

4. Based on company studies, the FDA determines a "highest no-effect level," the highest level of intake associated with no adverse toxicological effects in the most sensitive, longest duration, most relevant animal study.

5. The FDA then calculates an acceptable daily intake (ADI) level for the additive by dividing the "highest no-effect level" by a "safety factor," which is often taken to be 100.

This process is usually a long, complex, and expensive procedure for a company. It is not unusual for that procedure to take up to 10 years or more before a decision is reached.

Since lethal compounds never make it very far in the approval process, the primary concern usually is whether the test compounds are likely to cause mutagenic, teratogenic, or other effects that could promote cancers in experimental animals or their offspring. (Mutagenic effects are those that result in mutations; teratogenic effects are those that cause birth defects.) The Food Additives Act of 1958 included a provision dealing with this issue, popularly known as the Delaney Amendment after James Delaney, the New York congressman who proposed it. The Delaney Amendment said that no chemical could be used as a food additive if it caused cancer in experimental animals in any amount whatsoever.

Suppose, for instance, that a chemical being studied caused cancer in rats if fed in amounts of 50 grams per day. That amount would almost certainly be far more than any human would consume if the chemical were used as a food additive. Nonetheless, the chemical would be prohibited from use as a food additive because of its effect on rats. The amendment is sometimes called a zero tolerance regulation because it does not permit *any* harmful effects from a chemical. The philosophy behind the Delaney Amendment was that one can never really be certain whether or not a chemical will cause cancer in a person 20, 30, or more years after it has been ingested, even in very small amounts. If the chemical *ever* causes cancer in an experimental animal, Delaney says, it should not be considered for use in foods that humans consume.

The Delaney Amendment was modified by the Food Quality Protection Act of 1996, which relaxed the standard for the use of chemical as pesticides, but not for food additives. Critics of the Delaney Amendment suggest that the new standard dictated for pesticides—"reasonable certainty of no harm"—is a more realistic criterion to be used for proposed food additives. But the amendment still sets the standard for chemicals proposed for use as food additives, even though many individuals think that it is too harsh.

## Safety of Food Additives

The FDA and comparable agencies in other countries have made significant efforts to make sure that chemicals added to foods will not cause health problems for humans who consume those foods. Consumers can be almost certain that the additives used to preserve foods, give it color and flavor, and impart other desirable properties will not kill people, cause cancer, affect the health of their children, or result in other health problems.

Still, food additives are not absolutely risk free. The primary medical concern about the addition of chemicals to our food is the likelihood that some small fraction of the population will experience side effects. For example, some small and unknown fraction of the population is allergic to one or more of the common food additives. Some individuals are allergic to color and/or flavor additives, to preservatives like sulfites, to polysorbates, and to almost any other synthetic food additive that one can name. The side effects produced by these additives range from rashes and hives to headaches and nausea. It is only in the rarest cases that these side effects become life threatening, although the discomfort they produce can be serious for those who experience them. The chart on page 50 summarizes some common allergies to food additives.

One group of additives that does pose a potentially serious health threat is the nitrites, compounds widely used to preserve meats and to retain their pinkish-red color. When used as food additives, nitrites can undergo chemical changes that result in the formation of relatively dangerous compounds. The problematic reaction occurs when the nitrite group ($NO_2$) reacts with an amino group ($NH_2$) from the protein found in meat. The product of that reaction is a nitrosamine, a compound containing the $=N-N=O$ group. An example of a nitrosamine is shown in the diagram below.

Nitrosamines are well-known carcinogenic agents, therefore, nitrites would normally not be permitted for use as food additives. But nitrites continue to be approved by the FDA because they are so effective in preventing the growth of *Clostridiium botulinum,* the deadly bacterium that causes botulism. Industry specialists say that no satisfactory substitute for nitrites is yet available.

The search for new chemicals to be used as food additives continues today. Food technologists always seem to be able to imagine one more way of making our foods safer to eat or more attractive to purchase. For example, a research team at the University of Melbourne in Australia announced in 1999 the development of

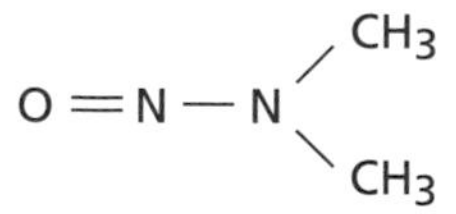

$$O = N - N \begin{array}{c} CH_3 \\ CH_3 \end{array}$$

**N-nitrosodimethylamine**

© Infobase Publishing

Chemical structure of N-nitrosodimethylamine

## ◄ ALLERGIC REACTIONS TO SOME COMMON FOOD ADDITIVES ►

| FOOD ADDITIVE | ALLERGIC REACTION(S) |
| --- | --- |
| aspartame | skin rash, hives, swelling of body tissue |
| benzoic acid/parabens | asthma, hives, swelling of the skin |
| cochineal | reactions ranging from hives to anaphylactic shock |
| FD&C Yellow No. 5 | hives |
| lactose | digestive problems (for people who are lactose intolerant) |
| monosodium glutamate (MSG) | headache; tightness in the chest, neck, and face |
| mycoprotein | nausea, vomiting, diarrhea, hives |
| sulfites | hives and itchiness of the skin; lung irritation; asthma |

an additive that can be used to reduce tooth decay. The product, named Recaldent, is a mixture of two substances, casein phospho-peptide (CPP) and amorphous calcium phosphate (ACP). CPP is derived from casein, a protein found naturally in milk, where it holds in suspension the calcium and phosphate ions from which tooth enamel is built. When Recaldent is added to foods, chewing gum, toothpaste, or similar products, it appears to protect teeth against tooth decay and to repair teeth where decay has already begun to occur.

The use of food additives dates to the earliest stages of human history. Until recently, almost the only use for additives was the preservation of foods. In the past century, additives have been developed for a variety of other purposes, perhaps the most important of which is for nutritional purposes. The invention of synthetic vitamins and minerals has made possible the enrichment of foods with nutritional additives, resulting in a dramatic decrease in nutritional disorders that have plagued humans for millennia. A major emphasis in additive research today is the development of chemicals that improve the attractiveness of food by augmenting its color, odor, taste, texture, shelf life, or other properties. Food chemistry is one of the most exciting fields of chemical research today, offering researchers challenges of creating even more useful and attractive additives for use in tomorrow's foods.

# 3
# SYNTHETIC FOODS

Of all the many accomplishments of food chemists in recent decades, perhaps the most remarkable is the development of synthetic foods. The term *synthetic food* refers to a food not found in nature. Non-dairy creamer, mentioned in chapter 1, is often cited as a classic example of a synthetic food. It does not exist anywhere in the natural world and was invented by food chemists to replace a natural product, natural cream. Any local grocery store contains many examples of synthetic foods, ranging from soft drinks to instant breakfast preparations to artificial eggs. The nutritional value of synthetic foods is the subject of intense debate today among nutrition experts and the general public.

Defining a synthetic food is not as simple as the preceding paragraph might suggest. Most foods sold today can be classified on a continuum ranging from completely natural to totally synthetic. The organic produce section of a market usually contains a number of fruits and vegetables that are truly natural; they have not been treated or altered in any way. Most other food products in the market have been modified to some extent or another. Table salt, for example, seldom consists of pure sodium chloride, as it is found in nature. It often contains at least one other component, potassium iodide, added for nutritional reasons. Many food products lie at the synthetic end of the continuum. Non-dairy creamer, for example, is not entirely synthetic because it contains natural substances, such as grain or vegetable oil. But the majority of components are inorganic compounds that one normally does not associate with a natural food.

Synthetic foods are attractive to both consumers and food producers for at least three reasons: convenience, storability, and cost. Many families today eat their meals "on the run" and want dinners that can be prepared quickly and with little effort. They prefer not to have to broil a piece of meat or fish, cook a few potatoes and vegetables, and prepare a dessert. Most synthetic foods can be heated and served quickly. Because they tend to contain fewer natural products, synthetic foods can also be kept on store and kitchen shelves for longer periods of time. They are ready to buy and serve at a moment's notice. Most synthetic foods also tend to be less expensive than natural foods. Non-dairy creamer, as an example, contains both natural and synthetic materials that cost only a few pennies per serving, compared to the greater cost of natural cream obtained from a cow.

The debate over synthetic foods today is not so much the extent to which they are artificial, but the nutritional effects they have on people who eat them. Is the savings in time and money offered by synthetic foods worth the health costs that may be traced to their consumption? Perhaps the simplest of all such cases to consider involves foods that are as nearly totally synthetic as possible: sweetened carbonated soft drinks, *artificial sweeteners,* and artificial fats.

## The Ultimate Synthetic Food: Soda Pop

Carbonated soft drinks made primarily of water containing dissolved carbon dioxide, artificial coloring, artificial flavoring, and other ingredients go by many different names in different parts of the country: pop, soda, soda pop, and tonic. These drinks are also widely known as soft drinks, although that term is generally used for noncarbonated drinks also.

Soda pop may well be one of the world's first totally artificial foods. Its chemical composition is, on the one hand, very simple. The sparkling taste that gives soda pop its distinctive feeling on the tongue results from carbonic acid ($H_2CO_3$), formed when carbon dioxide dissolves in water. The color and flavor of the drink come from (usually) artificial compounds, chemicals such as organic esters and aldehydes, developed by food chemists to mimic the flavors and odors of natural fruits and other plants. The drink's complexity arises from the precise kinds and proportion of additives used. Some soft drink companies emphasize that the secret of their products' success comes from a special recipe developed by the company that remains a proprietary secret. But that secret is almost always a list of artificial chemicals whose precise proportion results in some distinctive taste.

Soda water, unflavored water charged with carbon dioxide gas, was probably first prepared by the English physicist and chemist Joseph Priestley (1733–1804). In his 1772 paper, "Impregnating water with fixed air" ("fixed air" as the original name for carbon dioxide), Priestley described the product of this reaction as having a "delicate, agreeable flavor" that was "brisk and acidulous." He predicted that it would be "most agreeable to the stomach." Priestley even indicated that the addition of carbonated water to beer that had gone "flat" would restore its original effervescence without in any way affecting its flavor.

The first successful commercial production of carbonated soft drinks can be traced to the 1790s. A German watchmaker and inventor by the name of Jean Jacob Schweppe (1740–1821) tried to duplicate the medicinal spa waters that so many Europeans at the time depended on to cure their physical ailments. He developed a water–carbon dioxide mixture that those who tasted seemed to enjoy, and in 1783 he opened a small factory to bottle his product. In an ad published in 1798, Schweppe was the first person to use the term *soda water.*

In the United States, the first patent for the manufacture of "imitation mineral waters" in the United States was granted to an Englishman, Joseph Hawkins, in 1809. Hawkins and a partner by the name of Cohen established a company, the Philadelphia Mineral Water Association, to make and sell carbonated beverages. But the company soon failed.

Interest in soda waters grew slowly in the United States, their popularity growing primarily because such drinks were promoted as tonics that would cure disorders and improve one's general health.

Pharmacists and home brewers concocted beverages that contained not only water and carbon dioxide but also a variety of natural products considered healthful, such as birch bark, plant roots ("root beer"), sarsaparilla, and fruit extracts.

Arguably the most important long-term invention in the early history of soda pop in the United States occurred in 1886. In that year, an Atlanta druggist named John Styth (Stith) Pemberton (1831–88) invented a new drink that eventually became known as Coca-Cola. The ingredients of the drink included caffeine, vanilla extract, extract of coca leaves, citric acid, lime juice, sugar, oil of orange, oil of lemon, oil of nutmeg, oil of cinnamon, oil of coriander, oil of neroli, and alcohol. Pemberton brewed this concoction over a fire in his back yard and marketed it as a brain and nerve tonic in his drugstore and others.

Pemberton's business grew slowly at first, with sales averaging no more than a dozen drinks per day, grossing less than $50 in the first year (compared to advertising costs of $73.96). Pemberton's bookkeeper, Frank Robinson, suggested the name *Coca-Cola* because it alluded to two of the three most potent ingredients in the drink, coca leaves and kola nuts, from which the caffeine was obtained. (The third potent ingredient was, of course, alcohol.) Like so many other patent medicines available at the time, this early formulation probably *did* make people feel better—not because it cured any diseases or physical disorders but because it contained cocaine, caffeine, and alcohol.

Today, Coca-Cola is one of the largest and most successful businesses in the world, producing dozens of soft drinks in nearly 200 different nations. It reported a net income of $5.08 billion in 2006 on total sales of $24.09 billion worldwide. Of course, Coca-Cola is by no means the only soda pop available to consumers today. Many other brands have been developed to take advantage of the appeal of carbonated soft drinks.

## Soda Pop and Nutrition

In recent years, some people have criticized soda pop on nutritional grounds. They argue that it scarcely deserves to be called a food since it typically contains few, if any, nutrients. As noted earlier, soda pop consists of water, dissolved carbon dioxide, artificial flavoring, artificial coloring, and other ingredients. Chief among these other ingredients is sugar or sugar substitutes. Perhaps ironically, it is sugar and other caloric sweeteners—arguably the most "natural" ingredients in soda pop—that attract the most criticism.

Soda pop has become one of the most popular beverages purchased regularly by consumers, especially by children and young adults. Study after study has shown that consumers in general, and children and young adults in particular, have moved from milk to soda pop as their beverage of choice. For example, the 2006 *Statistical Abstract* of the United States shows that per capita consumption of all types of milk in the United States has fallen from 27.6 gallons per year in 1980 to 21.6 gallons in 2003, a decrease of 22 percent. By contrast, per capita consumption of carbonated soft drinks has risen from 35.1 gallons per year in 1980 to 46.4 gallons in 2003, an increase of 32 percent.

Many nutritionists are concerned about these trends, warning of the health risks of replacing milk with carbonated beverages. Soft drink companies respond by pointing out that soda pop is not, in and of itself, a harmful beverage. In fact, they say, it does have health benefits. The Coca-Cola Company, for example, says on its Web site that soft drinks can contribute to a healthy diet in two ways. First, they provide the volume of water—about two liters (two quarts)—that every person needs every day to stay healthy. Second, soft drinks provide carbohydrates that provide the body with the quick energy it needs to function properly. Soda pop companies also point out that the amount of sugar and caffeine found in their products is not significantly greater, and often less than, that found in other popular beverages.

Some nutritionists respond that soft drinks are not inherently bad. For example, the American Dietetic Association's position is that "in moderation, soft drinks—like all foods—can fit into a healthful eating plan." The problem, the ADA points out, is that children and adults who drink soda pop are less likely to drink beverages that are more healthful, such as milk and fruit juices. In their position statement on the topic, the ADA concludes with the following suggestion: "There's no need to eliminate soft drinks, but try to get the nutrients you need from other sources. And, don't forget to watch your overall calorie intake."

Other nutritionists take stronger positions on the increasing consumption of soda pop by children and young adults. The Center for Science in the Public Interest (CSPI) points out, for example, that carbonated beverages now constitute the single largest source of refined sugar in the American diet. The average teenage boy now gets about 15 teaspoons of sugar a day from carbonated soft drinks, and the average girl, about 10 teaspoons of sugar a day. These amounts are about equal to the *total* amount of refined sugar in a teenager's daily diet, as recommended by the U.S. Department of Agriculture.

Under these circumstances, the consumption of carbonated soft drinks may be one important factor in the growing problem of obesity among both adults and children seen in the United States today. While soda pop accounts for about 8–9 percent of all the calories consumed by the average U.S. teenager (including those who drink no carbonated soft drinks at all), that figure rises to about 18 percent among the top 10 percent of those who drink soda pop. A fair question might be to what extent (if at all) soda pop consumption is contributing to weight problems among at least some portion of this group of teenagers.

Refined sugar may be implicated in health problems other than obesity. One of the most serious of those problems may be heart disease, currently the number one cause of death among adults in the United States. Many clinicians now believe that high consumption of sugar may contribute to the development of heart disease.

In addition, the position that carbonated soft drinks do no serious harm when included in an otherwise healthy diet, while probably correct, ignores the fact that many individuals substitute soda pop for more healthful beverages. The most obvious "loser" in this equation is milk, whose consumption tends to drop off as the consumption of soda pop increases. As young children and adolescents drink less milk, they tend to consume less of the calcium they need to build strong bones and teeth, increasing long-term risks of osteoporosis and other bone disorders.

Finally, in a small percentage of cases, the consumption of soda pop may actually pose a health risk to certain individuals. For example, caffeine, an ingredient in five of the six most popular soda pops, causes nervousness, irritability, sleeplessness, and rapid heart beat. And certain food additives used to add color or flavor to a drink may also cause allergic reactions among certain individuals.

The carbonated soft drink industry poses, therefore, a classic problem for those interested in promoting good nutrition among children and adults. The nutritional value of such foods is questionable, while their commercial profitability is significant. The dilemma nutritionists face is how to promote good dietary practices in the face of very large and aggressive advertising campaigns by a prosperous industry whose major concerns are not necessarily those of encouraging such practices.

## Caloric Sweeteners

Sweeteners can be classified into two general groups: caloric (or nutritive) and noncaloric (or non-nutritive) products. Caloric sweeteners are natural products, such as sucrose, fructose, glu-

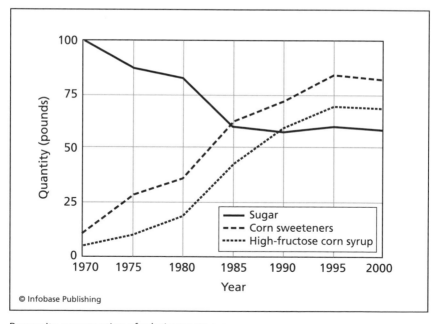

© Infobase Publishing

Per capita consumption of caloric sweeteners

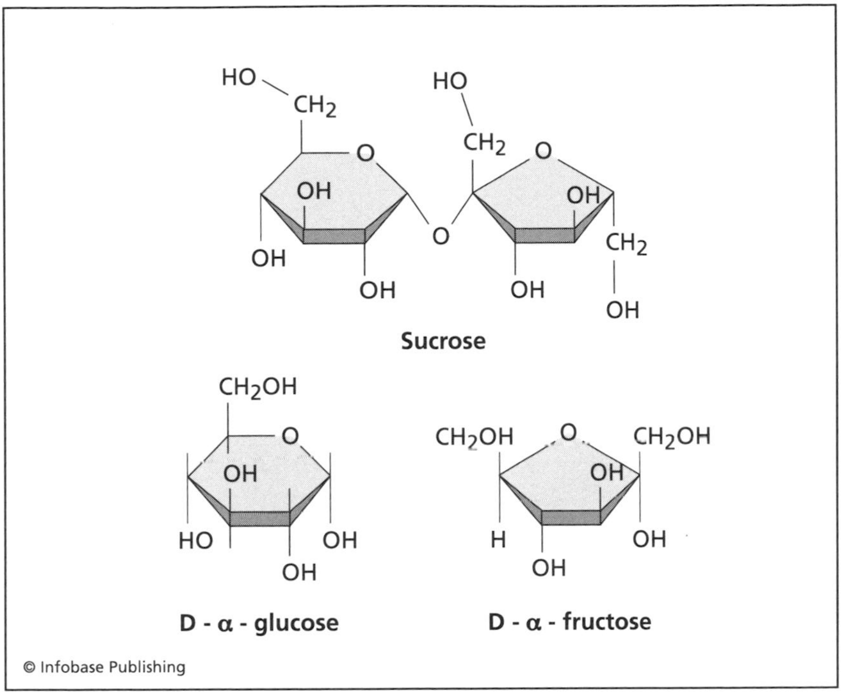

Chemical structures of three sugars: sucrose, glucose, and fructose

cose, sorbitol, and mannitol, that provide between 2.6 and 4 *calories* per gram. Noncaloric sweeteners are synthetic products, such as saccharine and aspartame, that provide very few or no calories. Noncaloric sweeteners are also called artificial sweeteners or sugar substitutes. The graph on page 58 shows trends in the consumption of sugar and other sweeteners in the United States from 1980 to 2003. The graph shows trends in consumption of three kinds of sweeteners: refined sugar from sugarcane and sugar beets; corn sweeteners, which include glucose and dextrose; and high-fructose corn syrup.

Unless otherwise indicated, the term *sugar* usually refers to the disaccharide sucrose, whose chemical structure is shown above. Disaccharides consist of two molecules of one or more simple sugars bonded to each other. The two components of sucrose are two molecules of glucose (also known as dextrose, grape sugar, or corn sugar). When a molecule of sucrose is metabolized, it produces two molecules of glucose, the molecule primarily responsible for the release of energy in the human body:

$$C_{12}H_{22}O_{11} + H_2O \rightarrow 2C_6H_{12}O_6$$

sucrose            glucose

Glucose is a monosaccharide, the simplest type of sugar. Although *glucose* is the name chemists prefer, it is frequently referred to as dextrose. The structural formula of glucose is shown on page 59, with that of sucrose. It is obtained commercially from the hydrolysis of corn starch or other cellulose-containing materials, with either acids or enzymes used as catalysts in the reaction.

High-fructose corn syrup (HFCS) is a liquid mixture of glucose and fructose made by treating glucose-rich corn syrup with enzymes. Fructose occurs naturally in many kinds of fruit and is also known as fruit sugar or levulose. It is very desirable as a sweetener because it is about 75 percent sweeter than sucrose. High-fructose corn syrup may contain anywhere from about 42 to 99 percent fructose. Fructose is a monosaccharide with a chemical structure very similar to that of glucose. The structural formula for fructose is shown on page 59 with that of sucrose and glucose. Many nutrition experts classify HFCS as a synthetic food because it is produced by industrial means and is not a natural product itself.

HFCSs first became commercially available in 1967, but they did not become widely popular until the late 1970s. This increase in popularity came about when makers of the sweetener significantly increased the concentration of fructose in HFCS mixtures. As a result, HFCSs became highly desirable as substitutes for both sucrose and glucose in soft drinks, jams and jellies, confectionery products, frozen desserts, condiments, bakery products, and canned fruits and juices. The substitution of HFCSs for sucrose and glucose in food products has raised concerns among nutritionists, however, because they may contribute to the increasing amount of sweet foods in the average American's diet.

In fact, health concerns about the growing proportion of sweet foods in the American diet have led to greater interest in the use of artificial sweeteners as substitutes for glucose, fructose, and sucrose in processed foods. The other important reason for such interest is the problem of diabetes, the inability of some persons to metabolize glucose. An excess or deficiency of glucose in a diabetic's diet is not just a long-term concern; it can lead to serious short-term health problems, including coma and death.

# Artificial Sweeteners

Some people regard artificial sweeteners as the way to avoid the health problems associated with caloric sweeteners such as sugar and HFCS. These synthetic foods add no calories or virtually no calorics to a person's diet. As of late 2004, the U.S. Food and Drug Administration (FDA) had approved five artificial sweeteners for use in the United States. They are saccharin, aspartame, sucralose, acesulfame potassium, (abbreviated as acesulfame-K), and neotame. A sixth artificial sweetener, tagatose, was confirmed in 2001 as a generally recognized as safe (GRAS) chemical. Tagatose is derived from lactose and is present in small amounts in dairy products and other natural sources. Two other products are currently under FDA review, alitame and cyclamates. Cyclamates were once FDA approved, but approval was withdrawn in 1970.

Decisions about the use of artificial sweeteners vary from nation to nation. For example, alitame is currently approved for use in Australia, New Zealand, Mexico, and China. Some artificial sweeteners approved for use in foreign countries, but not the United States, include dihydrochalcones (European Union and Zimbabwe) and thaumatin (Israel, Japan, European Union, Australia, and New Zealand).

Artificial sweeteners tend to taste much sweeter than do natural sugars. The chart on page 62 shows the relative sweetness of various sugar substitutes. Relative sweetness is measured by comparing the taste of a 4 percent water solution of the substance compared to a sucrose solution of comparable concentration.

## SACCHARIN

Saccharin was the first artificial sweetener to be discovered. It was identified in 1879 when Johns Hopkins researchers Constantine

## ◄ RELATIVE SWEETNESS OF VARIOUS ARTIFICIAL SWEETENERS ►

| ARTIFICIAL SWEETENER | RELATIVE SWEETNESS |
|---|---|
| sucrose | 1.0* |
| tagatose | 1.0** |
| cyclamates | 30* |
| HFCS | 100–160*** |
| aspartame | 180* |
| acesulfame K | 200* |
| saccharin | 300–500* |
| sucralose | 600* |
| hernandulcin | 1,000* |
| alitame | 2,000** |
| thaumatin | 3,000* |
| Neotame | 7,000–13,000** |

Sources: *Ben Selinger. *Chemistry in the Marketplace,* 4th ed. Sydney: Harcourt Brace Jovanovich, 1989, Table 11.5, page 428.
**CalorieControl.org. "Low-Calorie Sweeteners." Available online. URL: http://www.caloriecontrol.org/lowcal.html. Downloaded September 10, 2006.
***Food Resource. "Sugar Sweetness." Oregon State University. Available online. URL: http://food.oregonstate.edu/sugar/sweet.html. Downloaded September 10, 2006.

Fahlberg and Ira Remsen were developing new food preservatives. It is said that Fahlberg accidentally spilled one of the substances being studied onto his hand. Some time later, he noticed that the substance tasted sweet and began to consider marketing the product as an artificial sweetener. Fahlberg and Remsen jointly published a paper describing their work, but Fahlberg went on to request a patent for the discovery without Remsen's knowledge. He eventually became very wealthy from proceeds of the discovery, none of which he shared with Remsen. (Remsen was later quoted as saying, "Fahlberg is a scoundrel. It nauseates me to hear my name mentioned in the same breath with him.") The product was first manufactured by the chemical company Monsanto and was the company's first commercial product. Two years after its founding in 1901, Monsanto was shipping all of the saccharin it produced to the Coca-Cola Company for use in its soft drinks.

Saccharin belongs to the chemical family known as the sulfimides. Its systematic name is o-benzosulfimide, or benzoylsulfonic imide. It is a white crystalline solid that is usually sold in the form of its sodium salt under the name Sweet'N Low or Sugar Twin. Saccharin's structural formula is shown below.

Controversy has surrounded saccharin throughout its existence. As early as 1907, one government food safety official tried to ban the substance from food. President Theodore Roosevelt branded that official "an idiot," however, and the product remained on the market.

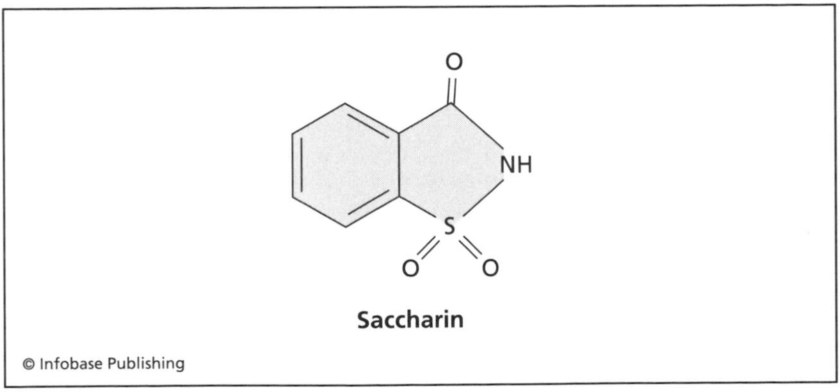

**Saccharin**

© Infobase Publishing

Chemical structure of saccharin

### ◄ IRA REMSEN (1846–1927) ►

Ira Remsen's name is familiar to any historian of American science today. He is best remembered for two accomplishments: the first was the discovery in 1879 of o-benzoyl sulfimide, the compound now known as saccharin, and his contributions to the development of professional education in science in the United States.

Ira Remsen was born in New York City on February 10, 1846, of Dutch and Huguenot ancestry. At his parents' urging, he earned his medical degree from Columbia University's College of Physicians and Surgeons in 1867. He worked briefly as a practicing physician, and then decided to pursue the subject that interested him: chemistry. He spent a year at the University of Munich before transferring to the University of Göttingen, where he studied with the eminent German chemist Rudolph Fittig (1835–1910). He then followed Fittig to the University of Tübingen, where he worked as Fittig's assistant for two years. In 1870 he was awarded his Ph.D. in chemistry.

Remsen was appointed professor of chemistry at Williams College in 1872, but he found that the institution was not eager to support his own research or his "new" methods of teaching chemistry. Remsen was eager, therefore, to receive an offer to move to Johns Hopkins in 1876, where he was encouraged to install his new approach to the teaching of science.

Remsen is probably best known by many people for his discovery with Constantin Fahlberg of saccharin. Fahlberg, a Russian chemist, had come to Johns Hopkins University to do postdoctoral research with Remsen on the development of new chemical food preservatives. During this research, Remsen and Fahlberg accidentally discovered a new compound, o-benzoyl sulfimide, that was much sweeter than natural sugar. Four years later, after Fahlberg had left Johns Hopkins, he applied for a patent for the

Four years later, a group of federal scientists decided that saccharin was an "adulterant" whose use was to be controlled by the government. Its use was then restricted to food products designed for use by invalids.

Restrictions on saccharin's use in foods were briefly lifted during World War I. Sugar was in short supply during the war, and the government decided to allow food processors to use saccharin in its place. After the war, saccharin use began to drop as supplies of natu-

compound, which he named *saccharin,* after the Latin word for "sweet," *saccharum.* Fahlberg did not include Remsen's name on the patent, and the Johns Hopkins chemist never received any financial profit from the discovery.

But Remsen's contributions in the area of science education are, in some respects, at least as important as those resulting from the discovery of saccharin. He came to the newly established Johns Hopkins University in 1876 with a passion for introducing German methods of laboratory instruction, an aspect of science education that was essentially missing from most college classrooms in the United States at the time. His skills at teaching and encouraging young students soon brought many of the most able students in chemistry to Johns Hopkins for their graduate studies. In 1901, Remsen was chosen to become the second president of the university, serving until 1913. In addition to his work at Johns Hopkins, Remsen authored three widely used texts, *Inorganic Chemistry, Organic Chemistry,* and *Theoretical Chemistry,* and founded the *American Chemical Journal,* of which he was editor for 35 years.

During his 12 years at Johns Hopkins, Remsen proved to be an efficient and effective administrator, expanding the university's curriculum and overseeing an ambitious building program. In addition to his labors at Johns Hopkins, Remsen served the nation as chair of a national committee on the control of food products and their adulteration, under President Theodore Roosevelt. After his retirement from the university in 1912, he continued to serve as a consultant to industry until his death in Carmel, California, on March 4, 1927. In 1927, Johns Hopkins named its new chemistry building in his honor, Remsen Hall. His ashes are interred in a wall of the building behind a plaque in his honor.

ral sugar became more readily available. In 1958, Congress passed the Food Additives Amendment to the Food, Drug, and Cosmetic Act (the act that included the Delaney Clause), which directed the FDA to categorize known food additives. The FDA listed saccharin as "generally recognized as safe" (GRAS), precluding further governmental regulation on its use.

Saccharin underwent its most serious testing challenges in the 1970s. During that decade, the FDA began an examination of many substances listed as GRAS. One group of studies suggested that saccharin was not entirely safe and may even cause bladder cancer in experimental animals (rats). Although those carcinogenic effects were later blamed on impurities in the saccharin used in the studies, the compound remained on the FDA's list of regulated additives throughout the decade.

An especially damaging study was reported in 1977 by Canadian researchers led by D. L. Arnold. Like the FDA researchers, the Canadian team also reported elevated levels of bladder cancer in rats fed saccharin; it also confirmed that the result could be obtained with saccharin free of impurities. That year Congress passed a law banning the use of saccharin in foods except for special circumstances (such as prescription products for diabetics). That "temporary" ban lasted for 14 years. In 1991 the FDA withdrew its plans to ban saccharin, and over the next decade the product regained its place among legitimate and safe artificial sweeteners. In 2000, the National Toxicology Program removed saccharin from its *9th Edition of the Report on Carcinogens,* and President Bill Clinton signed a bill authorizing the removal of any warning messages on saccharin products.

## ASPARTAME

Serendipity, the act of making a useful discovery of something for which one is not actually searching, seems to be an inherent part of the discovery of nearly all artificial sweeteners. Like Remsen and Fahlberg's discovery of saccharin, the discovery of aspartame was accidental. James Schlatter, a chemist at the G. D. Searle pharmaceutical company, was involved in research on new drugs that might be used to treat ulcers. One day in December 1965, a small amount of one of the compounds with which he was working inadvertently got on his fingers. He did not notice what had happened until later, when he licked his finger to pick up a piece of paper. Immediately he noticed a strong, sweet taste. He eventually realized that the taste must have come from the compound he was working with that day, L-aspartylphenylalanine methyl ester. Abandoning normal laboratory safety procedures, he added some of the compound to a cup of black coffee. He drank it and found that the chemical did, indeed, have a very strong sweet flavor with none of the bitter aftertaste associated with saccharin. Schlatter's research team immediately grasped the compound's commercial potential and convinced Searle to begin developing the new product for FDA approval. Within a short time, aspartame became a widely popular consumer product, surpassing the use of any other artificial sweetener then available.

Aspartame is the generic name for the chemical whose systematic name is α-L-aspartyl-L-phenylalanine methyl ester or 3-amino-N-(α-carboxyphenethyl)-succinamic acid N-methyl ester. Aspartame is marketed commercially under a variety of brand names, including Canderel, Equal, and NutraSweet. The chemical structure of aspartame is shown below.

As the formula shows, aspartame is a dipeptide, a molecule consisting of two amino acids—aspartic acid and phenylalanine—joined to each other by a peptide bond. When aspartame is metabolized, it forms three products: the two amino acids and methanol (methyl alcohol). Aspartic acid is a nonessential amino acid, that is, one that the human body can manufacture from metabolites obtained from other foods, while phenylalanine is an essential amino acid, that is, one that the body cannot make and must be obtained from foods. Aspartic acid plays a number of important roles in the body, including the synthesis of nucleic acids (DNA and RNA) and urea

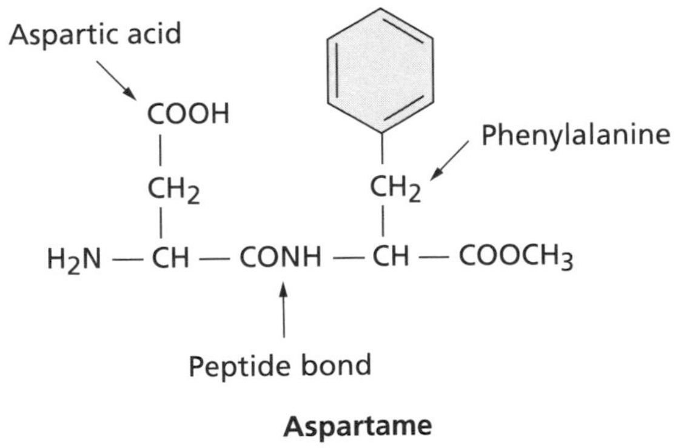

Chemical structure of aspartame

and the transmission of nerve messages in the brain. Phenylalanine plays a key role in the biosynthesis of other amino acids and some neurotransmitters. Both substances are totally natural components of the human body. Methanol by contrast, is highly toxic, but the amount produced during the metabolism of aspartame is so small as to be considered harmless.

The biochemistry of aspartame is different from that of saccharin. Saccharin passes through the digestive system without being digested at all. Since it undergoes no changes in the digestive system, saccharin produces no calories and is a truly "calorie-free" artificial sweetener.

By contrast, aspartame *is* digested and metabolized in the body. Like other amino acids, it provides 4 calories of energy per gram when metabolized. This production of energy is considered insignificant, however. The reason is that aspartame is so sweet that only very small amounts of the sweetener are needed to produce the same level of sweetness as a much larger amount of sugar. When aspartame is used to replace sugar, about 99.4 percent of the calories that would have been obtained from sugar are eliminated. Thus, while aspartame cannot be considered a "zero calorie" sweetener, it certainly qualifies as a very, very low calorie sweetener.

Controversy over the safety of aspartame began almost as soon as the FDA first granted approval for its use in certain types of foods (July 26, 1974). Less than a month later two concerned citizens, James Turner and Dr. John Olney, filed a petition objecting to the FDA's decision, citing possible errors in Searle's testing procedures. After continued studies, extending over a seven-year period, the FDA reiterated its original decision to approve aspartame for use in dry foods.

A year later, Searle requested FDA approval for the use of aspartame in carbonated beverages and certain other liquids. This time, the National Soft Drink Association (NSDA) raised objections with the FDA in spite of its potentially lucrative value to the association. The NSDA expressed concerns about the stability of aspartame in liquid solution under extremes of temperature and asked for further studies on aspartame's safety as an additive in carbonated beverages. The FDA was unconvinced by the NSDA's concerns and, in the fall of 1983, the first carbonated beverages containing aspartame went on the market.

NSDA's early concerns notwithstanding, aspartame has become an essential ingredient of many soft drinks. Since its introduction in 1981, aspartame has become by far the most popular sweetener in virtually all canned and bottled diet soft drinks in the United States. Carbonated soft drinks now account for an estimated 85 percent of all aspartame consumed in the United States.

Still, complaints about aspartame continue to pour in. A number of Internet Web sites are devoted to having the product banned by the FDA in connection with various reported adverse reactions to aspartame. The health problems ascribed to aspartame range from neurological and behavioral symptoms, such as headaches, dizziness, and mood alterations, to gastrointestinal symptoms, alterations in menstrual patterns, and allergic and/or dermatologic symptoms.

The Centers for Disease Control and Prevention (CDC) conducted an intensive study of some of these symptoms in 1984 and reported that the vast majority were mild and did not represent a serious long-term threat to human health. Everyone agrees, however, that aspartame *does* pose a health risk for individuals who have a genetic disorder known as phenylketonuria (PKU). People with PKU lack the enzyme needed to convert phenylalanine to tyrosine. As a consequence, any phenylalanine that they ingest is not metabolized but builds up in the bloodstream. Excessive amounts of the amino acid can damage the brain, leading to mental retardation. Because phenylalanine is a metabolic product of aspartame, all food products that contain aspartame are required to carry a warning that people with PKU should avoid the product.

## ACESULFAME-K, SUCRALOSE, AND NEOTAME

A third artificial sweetener, acesulfame was discovered accidentally in a manner similar to that as saccharin and aspartame: In 1967 Karl Claus, an employee of the large manufacturing company Hoechst AG, accidentally dipped his fingers into a chemical with which he was working in the laboratory. When he later licked his finger to pick up a piece of paper, he noted the very sweet taste of the chemical. This compound was later identified as acesulfame.

The systematic name for acesulfame is 6-methyl-1,2,3-oxathi-azine-4(3H)-one-2,2-dioxide. Its chemical structure is shown below.

The chemical structure of acesulfame is similar to that of saccharin (see on page 63). Acesulfame has one strongly ionizable hydrogen and usually occurs in the form of its potassium salt. The generic name for the product, acesulfame-K, is an abbreviation for that salt, acesulfame potassium. Acesulfame-K is sold commercially as an artificial sweetener under the names Sunette, Sweet One, or Swiss

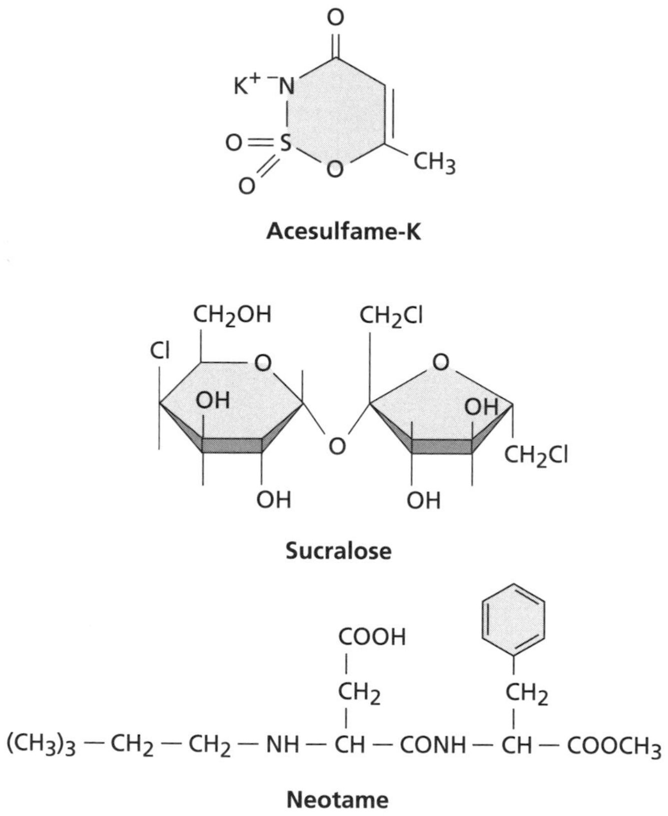

**Acesulfame-K**

**Sucralose**

**Neotame**

© Infobase Publishing

Chemical structures of three noncaloric sweeteners: acesulfame K, sucralose, and neotame

Sweet. The substance is a true no-calorie product since it is not digested or metabolized by the human body. It is excreted intact in the urine, except for the potassium ion, which is lost during its transit through the digestive system.

The FDA first approved acesulfame potassium for use in the United States in 1992, for production of gums and dry foods. Six years later, it was also approved for use in liquid foods, such as soft drinks. One of its first applications was in a new soft drink developed by the Pepsi Cola Company, called Pepsi ONE. Today, the chemical is used in over 1,800 different products in more than 40 countries worldwide.

Acesulfame potassium appears to have few, if any, disadvantages. It has a long shelf life (at least three years), does not break down at high temperatures, and has not yet been shown to be carcinogenic. Still, it has not yet proved to be especially popular as an artificial sweetener, especially compared with aspartame and saccharin. Its most popular applications are products in which it is combined with another artificial sweetener, usually aspartame. The advantage of the combination is that, while neither acesulfame nor aspartame by itself tastes quite like natural sugar, a combination of the two comes much closer to "the real thing."

Some products in which acesulfame-K can be found, either alone or in combination with aspartame, include beverages, such as Pepsi ONE, Diet Sprite, Diet Cherry Coke, Fresca, Diet V8, and Kraft Foods' Sugar-Free International Coffees and Crystal Light products; desserts and snacks, such as Jell-O Sugar Free Gelatin Desserts and Puddings, Hershey's Lite Chocolate Syrup, and Dreyer's No-Sugar-Added Ice Cream; and gums and candies, such as Trident Sugarless Gum, Starburst Fruit Twists, and Eclipse Polar Ice Gum. Pure acesulfame or an acesulfame–aspartame combination are also used in a variety of desserts, syrups, candies, sauces, yogurt, and alcoholic beverages.

One of the latest artificial sweeteners to be approved by the FDA was accepted in April 1998. Chemists produce sucralose by replacing three of the hydroxy groups in glucose with chlorine atoms, as shown in the formula on page 70. Its systematic name is 1,6-dichloro-1,6-dideoxy-$\beta$-D-fructofuranosyl-4-chloro-4-deoxy-$\alpha$-D-galactopyranoside. It is marketed commercially as a sugar substitute under the name Splenda. It is also used as a sweetening agent in more than 100 kinds of foods, including soft drinks, desserts, and dressings. As shown in the table on page 62, it is about 600 times as sweet as sucrose itself.

The discovery of sucralose is one of the most bizarre stories in the history of artificial sweeteners. In 1989, the British sugar company Tate & Lyle was looking for new ways to use sucrose, to increase demand for the product. They considered the possibility of using sucrose as an intermediary in a variety of chemical processes and asked Leslie Hough at King's College, London, to explore that possibility. Hough asked a foreign graduate student by the name of Shashikant Phadnis to begin testing certain derivatives of sucrose. Phadnis misunderstood Hough's directions, and began *tasting* those derivatives. In the process, Phadnis discovered the intense sweetness of the chlorinated derivatives of sucrose, and another new sweetener was found!

Sucralose has a number of desirable qualities as a sugar substitute. It does not have the bitter aftertaste associated with saccharin, and it has a much longer shelf life and heat stability than aspartame. No harmful side effects have as yet been announced and it is not digested or metabolized in the human digestive system, making it a true no-calorie sweetener.

FDA approval of neotame was announced in 2002, making it the latest of artificial sweeteners to be made commercially available in the United States. Research on neotame began in the mid-1990s as part of the Monsanto company's effort to improve its very popular aspartame sweetener. As discussed earlier in this chapter, aspartame breaks down during digestion into aspartic acid and phenylalanine, and phenylalanine poses a health risk to individuals with phenylketonuria (PKU). The new research project was designed to find a product with aspartame's benefits but fewer of its disadvantages.

The solution to this problem was discovered by two French Monsanto researchers, Claude Nofre and Jean-Marie Tinti. Nofre and Tinti found that they could replace the terminal hydrogen on the aspartic acid end of the aspartame molecule with a 3,3-dimethylbutyl group. Compare the structure of neotame in the figure on page 70 with that of aspartame on page 67. The advantage of this arrangement is that it blocks the action of peptidases, enzymes that break down peptides. When ingested, a neotame molecule hydrolyzes to release methanol, as does aspartame, but the aspartame-like dipeptide remains intact. The dipeptide is excreted unchanged, releasing no phenylalanine to the bloodstream and producing no calories. The FDA reviewed 113 studies before approving neotame in 2002, having found no health effects from the product.

Monsanto has made an effort to assure consumers that the amount of methanol produced during the digestion of neotame is minuscule. One company press release, for example, points out that the amount of methanol resulting from the digestion of neotame is 200 times less than that in a sample of tomato juice of the same weight.

Chemically, neotame is N-[N-(3,3-dimethylbutyl)-L-$\alpha$-aspartyl]-L-phenylalanine 1-methyl ester. Its sweetness ranges from 7,000 to 13,000 times that of sucrose, depending on the formulation used. The product has been approved for use in baked goods, chewing gum, carbonated soft drinks, confections and frostings, refrigerated and non-refrigerated ready-to-drink beverages, tabletop sweeteners, frozen desserts and novelties, puddings and fillings, jams and jellies, yogurt-type products, toppings and syrups, and candies.

## Cyclamates and Alitame

As already noted, the FDA has approved five non-nutritive sweeteners just discussed: saccharin, aspartame, acesulfame-K, sucralose, and neotame. Others, however, have been developed and are under consideration by the FDA, the two most important of which are cyclamates and alitame. The discovery of the cyclamates yields yet another fantastic story in the history of artificial sweeteners. In 1937 Michael Sveda, then a graduate student at the University of Illinois, was carrying out research on the synthesis of antipyretic drugs (drugs that control fever). He was smoking at the time (a practice that would not be allowed today!) and, at one point, brushed some loose threads of tobacco from his lips. As he did so, he noticed a very sweet flavor on the cigarette. With a little thought and analysis,

# ◄ THE MONSANTO COMPANY ►

> *No single corporation has ever done greater*
> *damage to the planet than Monsanto.*
> —Rachel's Environment & Health Weekly, *Issue #504,*
> *July 25, 1996. Available online at http://www.rachel.*
> *org/bulletin/bulletin.cfm?Issue_ID=619*

Life is not always easy for the world's chemical manufacturers these days. Companies such as Monsanto, DuPont, Merck, Aventis, Merck, and Union Carbide are being blamed for a host of environmental problems and health problems among humans and other animals. Chemicals produced by these companies, ranging from food additives to genetically modified foods, are sometimes viewed not in terms of whatever benefits they can provide to people but as primarily tools by which corporations can generate huge profits for stockholders. As with most controversial issues, there is probably some truth as well as a good deal of mythology in these complaints.

In any case, one of the primary targets of criticisms about the chemical industry in general, and the manufacture of genetically modified foods in particular, is the Monsanto Company. Monsanto is about the 20th largest chemical corporation in the United States, and the largest company specializing in agrochemicals, chemicals used in agriculture. The company has long made an extraordinary effort to portray itself as a considerate business that strives to understand and respond to the needs of its customers and society in general. This concern is reflected in Monsanto's Pledge, first adopted in 1990, in which it promises to "respect and work with all interested parties, developing technology with benefits that are meaningful to farmers and consumers throughout the world, and only developing products that we are confident are safe and will provide value to our customers." The extent to which the company has actually accomplished the goals outlined in its pledge is a subject of some dispute, although it continues to refine, improve, and publicize its 1990 statement as a guiding principle in its operation.

The Monsanto company was founded in 1901 by John F. Queeny, the grandson of Irish immigrants. Queeny was forced to go to work at the age of 12 when the Great Chicago Fire of 1871 destroyed his father's real estate business. His first job was as a messenger boy for a drug company. Over the years, he remained in that business, slowly rising to more important positions. In 1901, he borrowed money to start his own business to manufacture products for the food and pharmaceutical industries. He named the company after his wife, Olga Mendez Monsanto. The first chemical produced by the company was the artificial sweetener saccharin. Queeny sold his entire output to a young soft drink company in Atlanta, Georgia, called the Coca-Cola Company.

Monsanto grew slowly over the years, adding new products and, eventually, buying up other companies. It started producing one of its most successful products, aspirin, in 1917 and continued to be the number 1 manufacturer of the drug until the mid-1980s. In the 1960s the company changed the focus of its operations and created its first distinct Agricultural Division. It introduced a number of new herbicides, the most successful of which were Lasso, Randex, Avadex, and Roundup. By 1962, the company's sales had passed the $1 billion mark for the first time in history.

Monsanto's research in the field of *recombinant DNA* began with a program in molecular biology established in 1980. That program eventually became the most extensive research effort in recombinant DNA agricultural products anywhere in the world. Monsanto researchers produced the first genetically modified cell in 1982, and a year later they grew the first genetically modified plants. In 1991, the company created a separate division called NatureMark to sell potatoes genetically engineered to resist insects. Two years later, Monsanto received approval for the sale of its first recombinant DNA product, bovine somatotropin (bST).

By the end of the 1990s, Monsanto was recognized as one of the world's leaders in the development and sale of genetically modified food products, including NewLeaf insect-protected potatoes; Bollgard insect-protected cotton; YieldGard rootworm-protected corn; Roundup Ready corn, soybeans, canola, and cotton; and the FlavrSavr tomato, a product that was approved for use but not made available commercially.

Company representatives speak with pride and assurance of Monsanto's commitment to the principles of its 1990 pledge. They note that in 2002 all of Monsanto's seed production sites in the United States and its quality assurance laboratory received 9002 certification from the International Organization of Standardization, an indication that the facilities had met certain clearly defined standards of customer attention, company leadership, a factual approach to decision making, continued improvement in business practices, and other desirable business qualities.

For whatever strengths and weaknesses it may have as a company, Monsanto has come to represent many of the difficult issues and controversies involved in the development, sale, and use of chemicals in the modern world.

Sveda was able to identify the source of that sweetness, a substance belonging to a class of compounds known as cyclamates.

Two cyclamates eventually found use as artificial sweeteners, sodium and calcium cyclamate. The generic term *cyclamate* is used for either of the two compounds. The structural formulas for sodium and calcium cyclamate are given below.

The two compounds are also known by a number of synonyms, most commonly sodium cyclohexylsulfamate and calcium cyclohexylsulfamate, respectively.

Sveda eventually applied for a patent for his discovery, which he later sold to Dupont. Dupont, in turn, sold the patent for cyclamates to Abbott Laboratories, which petitioned the FDA for approval of the sweetener in 1950. Abbott's initial interest in cyclamates was to mask the bitter taste of certain drugs it produced. The company later extended its petition to include the use of cyclamates as sweeteners for diabetics and others who had to limit their intake of sugar.

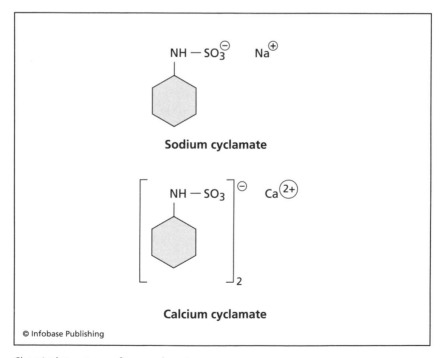

© Infobase Publishing

Chemical structures of two cyclamates

In 1958 the FDA approved Abbott's petition and listed cyclamates as a GRAS substance, making it available for use in a wide range of products. Almost immediately, soft drink manufacturers began to use cyclamates as a sweetener in their products, sometimes by itself and sometimes in association with saccharin.

The success of cyclamates in the artificial sweetener market was, however, short-lived. In 1969 a group of researchers reported that rats fed a diet that included the commercial sweetener Sucaryl were very likely to develop bladder cancer. Sucaryl is a mixture containing nine parts of cyclamate to one part of saccharin. Critics of the research questioned the value of the results, however, since the rats were fed an extraordinary amount of Sucaryl (equivalent to the quantity found in about 800 cans of soda pop) for nearly their whole lives. However, officials of the FDA were sufficiently concerned to ban the sale of cyclamates in the United States until further studies confirmed the product's safety for humans.

Those studies went on for more than a decade, culminating in a 1984 report by the Cancer Assessment Committee of the FDA that concluded that cyclamates are not carcinogenic. A year later, this finding was confirmed in an independent evaluation of the report by the National Academy of Sciences.

These studies have convinced regulatory agencies in a number of countries that cyclamates pose no threat to human health, and the product has now been licensed for use in more than 50 countries, including Canada, Denmark, Sweden, Belgium, the Netherlands, Switzerland, and Israel. The FDA is still considering its position on cyclamates, however. One ongoing concern is that, while the compounds may not actually cause cancer, they may promote the growth of cancers that develop in other ways.

Alitame is an artificial sweetener developed by chemists at the Pfizer pharmaceutical company in the 1980s. It is a dipeptide like aspartame except that it consists of the amino acids aspartic acid and alanine rather than aspartic acid and phenylalanine. Alitame has a number of advantages over aspartame. It is about 10 times as sweet as aspartame; it has no unpleasant aftertaste; it survives high temperatures better than aspartame; and, because it lacks phenylalanine, it presents no health hazards for people with phenylketonuria. Pfizer filed a petition with the FDA in 1986 seeking approval for alitame as a food additive, but as of 2006, no action has been taken on that petition. The compound is available under the brand name Aclame in a number of other countries, including Australia, Mexico, New Zealand, and the People's Republic of China.

The development of artificial sweeteners has been a great advantage for people with diabetes and those who are trying to control their weight. They make it possible for such individuals to enjoy sweet foods without worrying about harmful side effects, such as diabetic reactions and obesity. The use of artificial sweeteners is not entirely beneficial, however, as some products may cause allergic reactions ranging from the unpleasant but harmless to life threatening. Users of artificial sweeteners should be aware of potential health risks and use such products accordingly.

## Artificial Fats

The problems of sugar consumption notwithstanding, many nutrition experts believe that the most important health problems in the United States today stem from Americans' high intake of fats. Many Americans consume 40 percent or more of their daily dietary calories in the form of fats. The FDA, the American Heart Association, and other health agencies, however, recommend diets containing no more than about 30 percent of calories from fats (and less than 10 percent from saturated fats),

Concern about fat consumption arises because diets high in fat are highly correlated with a variety of cardiovascular disorders, including high blood pressure, atherosclerosis ("hardening of the arteries"), heart attack, coronary heart disease, congestive heart failure, and stroke. Cardiovascular disorders are currently the leading cause of death in the United States. The American Heart Association estimates that 61.8 million Americans have cardiovascular disease, resulting in more deaths in the United States than the next seven causes (including all forms of cancer) combined. It is hardly surprising, then, that food scientists are interested in developing synthetic foods that mimic the desirable characteristics of fats and eliminate all or most of their disadvantages.

Fats are a member of the biochemical family known as lipids. The lipids include a wide variety of compounds present in living organisms that are grouped together on the basis of a single physical property: They are soluble in organic solvents such as benzene, ether, chloroform, and carbon tetrachloride but are insoluble in water.

Fats and oils are chemically similar lipids that consist of glycerol, a trihydric (three -OH groups) alcohol, esterified with one or more fatty acids. The only difference between fats and oils is their physical state (fats are solid and oils are liquid) and the degree of

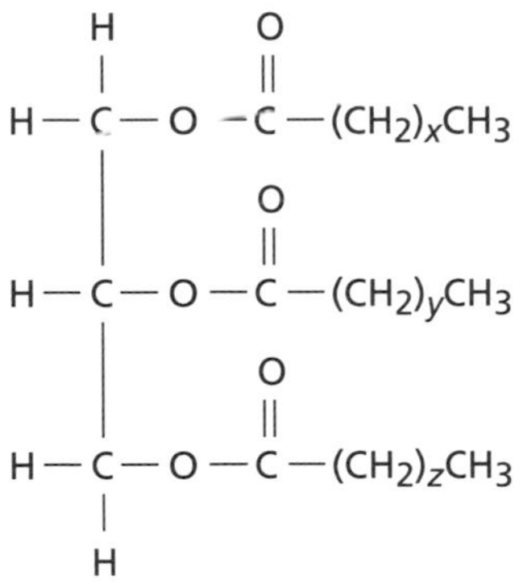

**A typical triglyceride**

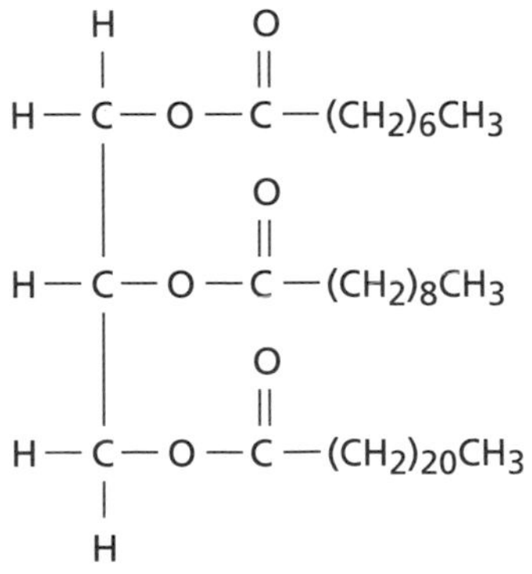

**Caprenin**

© Infobase Publishing

Chemical structures of a typical triglyceride and caprenin

unsaturation (the number of double bonds present) of the fatty acids they contain. The chemical structure of a typical fat is shown on page 79.

The three-carbon backbone at the left of the molecule is the remnant of the glycerol molecule from which the fat is formed. The three long-chain segments attached to the backbone are the remnants of the fatty acid from which it is formed. The fat shown here is also called a triglyceride because it has three (*tri-*) fatty acid remnants (*-glyceride*). Some fats contain only one fatty acid remnant (*monoglycerides*) and some contain only two fatty acid remnants (*diglycerides*). Fats that contain fatty acid remnants with double bonds are called *unsaturated fats,* while those that contain only single bonds are *saturated fats.*

A diet high in fat poses at least two risks to one's health. First, fats produce a relatively large amount of energy when metabolized, nine calories per gram, compared with four calories per gram for carbohydrates, like sugar and starch. Second, saturated fats are believed to be responsible for an increase in blood cholesterol levels which, in turn, have been implicated with an increased risk for heart disease.

The primary goal of food chemists in their search for synthetic fats is to modify lipid molecules so that they provide most of the sensory advantages possessed by fatty foods, the characteristics that make people *want* to eat fats, while reducing the risks posed by such molecules. The term *structured lipid* (SL) has been invented to describe lipids in which the position and character of fatty acid remnants in a lipid molecule have been altered from those found in the molecule's natural state.

One example of a structured lipid is a product known as caprenin, developed by Procter & Gamble (now P&G). As shown in the diagram on page 79, the caprenin molecule consists of the usual glycerol background to which are attached fatty acid remnants of 8, 10, and 22 carbon atoms, remnants corresponding to caprylic ($C_7H_{15}COOH$), capric ($C_9H_{19}COOH$), and behenic ($C_{21}H_{43}COOH$) acids. No molecule of this kind exists in nature, so it can legitimately be called a structured lipid. When this molecule is digested, the behenic acid formed is not metabolized but is absorbed by the body. Since only the glycerol, capric acid, and caprylic acid molecules formed are metabolized, fewer calories (5 calories per gram) are released compared with those obtained from a natural fat.

In 1991, Procter & Gamble filed a petition with the FDA, requesting that caprenin be considered a GRAS substance and that it be made available for commercial use. The SL's first application is in a proposed new candy bar, Mars Milky Way II, where caprenin replaces the cocoa butter used in the original version of the candy. On September 18, 2000, Procter & Gamble withdrew its GRAS petition, indicating that it might resubmit the application at a later date.

Another structured lipid product that has become commercially available is salatrim, developed by the Nabisco Foods Group. This SL is somewhat different from caprenin in that it consists of a mixture of glycerides containing four fatty acid fragments, rather than the three found in caprenin. The four fatty acids contain 2, 3, 4, and 18 carbon atoms. The comparable fatty acids are ethanoic ($CH_3COOH$), propanoic ($C_2H_5COOH$), butanoic ($C_3H_9COOH$), and stearic ($C_{17}H_{35}COOH$) acids. Salatrim's molecular structure gives it its name: Its molecules contain short- and long-chain acyl *triglyceride* molecules. Like caprenin, it has about half the calorie content of natural fats.

Nabisco notified the FDA in 1994 of its intention to seek approval for the use of salatrim as a GRAS substance. The introduction of GRAS substances in the marketplace involves a somewhat different approval process than that of other food additives. If a company's own research indicates that a new compound has no health effects on humans, it may notify the FDA that the compound can be considered "generally recognized as safe" (GRAS) and begin to market the compound commercially. The compound then remains on the FDA-approved GRAS list as long as objections are not raised or research presented to the FDA suggesting that the compound has been incorrectly classified as GRAS.

Thus, Nabisco began marketing salatrim under the brand name Benefat® shortly after notifying the FDA of the compound's GRAS status. It has thus far been used primarily in confectionery products, including chocolate chips and candies. A number of other SL products have been developed or are currently being studied in the United States and abroad. These include Structolipid (Pharmacia &

Upjohn AB, Sweden), Captex 810D (Abitec Corporation), Bohenin (Fuji Oil Company), and Neobee (Stepan Food Company).

Some nutrition groups have expressed concerns about the use of products such as caprenin and salatrim, arguing that data are insufficient to allow their release to the general public. In 1998, for example, the Center for Science in the Public Interest (CSPI) asked the FDA to deny Nabisco's petition to have salatrim listed as a GRAS substance. The CSPI pointed out that Nabisco had conducted only one short (28-day) study on the product, and this study had found some negative short-term effects of the product. The FDA has thus far not acted on either the original petition or CSPI's letter of complaint.

An entirely different approach in the production of a synthetic fat is olestra, perhaps the most famous fat substitute yet developed. Olestra was discovered in 1968 by Robert Volpenheim and Fred Mattson, researchers at Procter & Gamble's Miami Valley Laboratories. Volpenheim and Mattson were engaged in a project to develop a new kind of fat that could be digested more easily by premature babies. Instead, they came across a new compound that had many of the properties of a fat but that passed through the human body without being digested.

Olestra belongs to a group of compounds known as sucrose polyesters. These are compounds in which two or more hydroxyl groups in the sucrose molecule have been replaced by fatty acid fragments. Olestra is a mixture of the hexa-, hepta-, and octa-fatty acid esters of sucrose. In the diagram on page 83, each of the structures marked "FA" represents a fatty acid fragment substituted for a hydroxyl group on the sucrose molecule.

The molecule is so large that enzymes that normally digest sucrose (sucrases) have no access to the bonds on which they normally operate. As a result, the molecule passes through the human digestive system without being digested, absorbed, or metabolized.

The market appeal of olestra, then, is that it tastes like fat, but it contains no nutritional calories. For example, a one-ounce bag of potato chips normally contains about 10 grams of fat and 150 Calories. A comparable bag of chips made with olestra contains nearly the same amount of fat, 9 grams, but only 70 Calories (from constituents other than the fat). Olestra is marketed under the trade name Olean.

Chemical structure of olestra

Like other synthetic foods, olestra has a complex regulatory history. It began in 1975 when Procter & Gamble petitioned the FDA to approve olestra as a drug. The company took this approach because the compound seemed to be effective in lowering blood cholesterol. When the company was unable to provide sufficient evidence for this claim, however, it changed course. In 1987, Procter & Gamble submitted a new petition with the FDA, asking it to approve olestra as a food additive that could be substituted for up to 35 percent of the fats used in home cooking and 75 percent of the fats used in commercial food processing.

At this point the regulatory story becomes really complicated. P&G's original patent on olestra was due to expire in 1988, making it impossible for the company to complete its FDA application before losing its patent rights. Ultimately, it took a special act of Congress to extend P&G's patent and allow it to complete its application process with the FDA.

The FDA finally acted on P&G's petitions on January 24, 1996, when it granted approval for the use of olestra in a limited variety of commercial products, including potato chips, crackers, and tortilla chips. P&G and other food companies soon began marketing a variety of new commercial products containing olestra, including Fat Free Pringles, Wow Potato Chips, and Ruffles, Lay's, Doritos, and Tostitos MAX chips. A long-term goal of P&G is to obtain FDA approval to

# ◄ THE CENTER FOR SCIENCE IN THE PUBLIC INTEREST ►

*But who will watch the watchers?*
*—Juvenal (ca. 70–138 C.E.)*

In a democratic society like that of the United States, one function of the government is to protect its citizens from possible risks posed by large corporations. For example, the Food and Drug Administration is charged with the responsibility of watching over the foods, drugs, cosmetics, and other chemicals that are made available to Americans in the marketplace. Without this protection, it would be possible for companies and individuals to sell products that were useless (that did not perform the function for which they were advertised) or even dangerous (that caused harm to users).

But governmental agencies are not infallible. They make errors, just as individual humans make mistakes. So it is important that nongovernmental agencies exist to keep an eye on the regulators. In the United States, hundreds of such organizations exist, including such well-known examples as the American Civil Liberties Union, the Council for Excellence in Government, the Electronic Privacy Information Center, the National Resources Defense Council, and the Worldwatch Institute. In the area of food and drug policy, one of the most effective watchdog agencies has long been the Center for Science in the Public Interest (CSPI).

The CSPI was founded in 1971 by three scientists who had been working at Ralph Nader's Center for the Study of Responsive Law: Albert J. Fritsch, a chemist; James B. Sullivan, a meteorologist; and Michael F. Jacobson, a microbiologist. The guiding principle behind the organization was that, given an opportunity, some scientists would be willing to abandon their careers in the laboratory and devote all their energies to working on public-interest issues. The CSPI's early work reflected the diverse interests of its founders

use the product in many other types of foods as well, including doughnuts, cakes, cookies, pastries, pies, ice cream, french fries, fried chicken and fried seafood, grilled meats and vegetables, margarines, and cheeses.

and included projects on strip mining, nuclear power, toxic chemicals, highway development, air pollution, food additives, and nutrition. Results of the organization's research were published in a regular newsletter written by the three founders.

In 1977, Fritsch and Sullivan left the CSPI to pursue other interests. With only Jacobson left, the CSPI's focus shifted to areas of his own interest—food and nutrition—that have remained the organization's primary concern over the last 20 years. The original all-purpose newsletter also evolved into a more specialized publication, "Nutrition Action Healthletter," that increased in circulation from about 30,000 in 1980 to more than a million at the turn of the century.

As with most public service organizations, the CSPI has produced a number of educational materials, ranging from books to pamphlets to posters. The CSPI's current publications include *Is Our Food Safe?* (book); "Protecting the Crown Jewels of Medicine: A Strategic Plan to Preserve the Effectiveness of Antibiotics" (report); *Marketing Booze to Blacks* (book and video); "Citizen's Action Handbook on Alcohol and Tobacco Billboard Advertising" (handbook); and "Chemical Cuisine: CSPI's Guide to Food Additives" (URL: http://www.cspinet.org/reports/chemcuisine.htm).

The CSPI is especially active in communicating with the FDA and other regulatory agencies, expressing their concern about food safety and other issues. For example, the organization has petitioned the FDA to withhold approval for a number of food additives, including olestra and salatrim, and to require health warning statements in all television ads for such products.

The Center for Science in the Public Interest is one of the best known and most highly regarded consumer organizations working to protect Americans' food supply. The organization has been criticized, however, for acting like "food police" and frightening the general public with unwarranted claims of health risks in the food supply. In any case, the CSPI continues to act as an important balance to federal organizations responsible for regulating the nation's food.

Almost since olestra was first discovered, however, P&G has had to deal with complaints by public interest groups about possible health effects of the new substance. Shortly after the company filed its first petition with the FDA in 1987, the CSPI suggested in a letter to the FDA that P&G's testing of the new product was inadequate and failed to address health concerns. Over the next two decades, CSPI, other consumer groups, and many individuals continued to express concerns about the safety of olestra.

Critics attribute a variety of gastrointestinal complaints to the consumption of olestra. Symptoms cited include bloating, diarrhea, cramps, loose stools, and urgency of defecation. In addition, olestra apparently has the tendency to bind to certain essential biochemicals, preventing the human body from absorbing them. Among these biochemicals are fat-soluble vitamins (A, D, E, and K) and carotenoids, such as beta-carotene, lycopene, lutein, and zeaxanthin. In an attempt to resolve this problem, the FDA now requires food producers to add fat-soluble vitamins to products containing olestra.

The debate over olestra and other synthetic foods has hardly been resolved. Companies that manufacture artificial sweeteners and fat substitutes continue to promote the safety and health values of their products, arguing that their more extensive use can help improve the nutritional diets of the average American. At the same time, many organizations and individuals point out that the vastly increased availability of synthetic diet foods (such as aspartame, saccharin, caprenin, and olestra) has had no discernible impact on that very problem. As these supposedly nutritionally sound synthetic foods have become more available, the average American's nutritional health has continued to deteriorate, with more and more people confronting the very problems of weight that those foods were supposed to help solve. For example, the Center for Disease Control and Prevention's 2003–2004 National Health and Nutrition Examination Survey (NHANES) found that 66.3 percent of all adults studied could be classified as overweight and 32.2 percent as obese. These figures represent an increase of 18 percent and 40 percent, respectively, over similar data collected in a 1994 NHANES survey.

Food chemists have developed a number of synthetic foods with the potential for improving the quality of food available to Americans and people around the world. Artificial sweeteners and fat substitutes can be useful for diabetics, people who are trying to lose weight, and others concerned about maintaining a healthy diet. At the same time, this is not to ignore the potential health risks for some people who may be allergic to such products and may develop other health problems by using them.

The flurry of research on synthetic foods appears to have abated to some extent in the last decade. Relatively few artificial sweeteners and fat substitutes have appeared on the market during that time. But research on such products has certainly not come to an end. Food chemists will continue to search for new products with which to augment and improve peoples' diets.

# 4
# GENETICALLY
# MODIFIED FOODS

For more than two decades, food chemists around the world have been engaged in an exciting new project with the potential for dramatically remaking the human diet. A number of new food products have been invented that are called *genetically engineered, genetically modified,* or, simply, *GM* foods. Research on genetically modified foods belongs to a long, rich, and very productive line of research known as biotechnology.

Although widely used for decades, the term *biotechnology* has been defined in some very different ways. For example, the *Merriam Webster's Collegiate Dictionary* (Eleventh edition, 2003) defines biotechnology as "applications of biological science." More recently, the Biotechnology Industry Organization provided a more limited definition, "the use of biological processes to solve problems or make useful products" ("Guide to Biotechnology: Glossary," available online at http://www.bio.org/speeches/pubs/er/glossary.asp). Other definitions are even more restrictive, focusing on specific technologies, such as gene transfer or recombinant DNA processes; for instance, the Web-based "Glossary of Food-Related Terms" suggests this definition for biotechnology: "the use of biotechnical methods to modify the genetic materials of living cells so they will produce new substances or perform new functions." It is the last of these definitions that will be used in this chapter.

## History of Biotechnology

One of the earliest applications of biotechnology was probably the use of microorganisms to make certain types of foods. Evidence indicates that people first learned how to make beer, wine, and vinegar more than 6,000 years ago by promoting the fermentation of fruits, vegetables, and grains with yeasts. People have also leavened bread with yeasts and cultured cheese and yogurt with bacteria for many hundreds, if not thousands, of years. Until the late 19th century, such processes were often as much an art as a science since farmers, vintners, and other producers of food knew little about the biological and chemical reactions that took place during these processes and tended to rely on trial-and-error methods for improving the foods they manufactured.

By 1900, however, agricultural techniques became more scientific as farmers learned about and began to put into practice the theory of Mendelian genetics, developed by the Austrian monk Gregor Mendel (1822–84) nearly a half-century earlier. The new system of manipulating the traits of plants and animals by selecting for certain genetic qualities is still an important part of modern agricultural techniques and is responsible for the development of high-yield seeds, chickens that produce more eggs and cows that give more milk, and larger turkeys, cattle, and other food animals that contain a larger percentage of edible food. Many of these improvements contributed to a vast expansion of the quality and amount of food available to people in developing countries beginning in the 1940s, an event that has become known as the Green Revolution. In Mexico, as an example, the nation went from importing half of all the wheat it needed to feed its people in the 1940s to self-sufficiency in 1956 to being an exporter of a half-million tons of wheat by 1964.

Until the 1970s, however, all of the techniques used in agricultural biotechnology were essentially empirical practices, based on the manipulation of visible physical traits (such as disease resistance and yield) that scientists could control in designing and growing new crops and animals. A fundamental and revolutionary change occurred in the early 1970s, however, resulting to a significant extent in a series of experiments carried out by two American biochemists, Herbert Boyer (1936–   ) and Stanley Cohen (1922–   ). Boyer and Cohen learned how to insert the gene from one organism into the genome of a second organism, a process that has since become known as recombinant DNA.

## Recombinant DNA Research

The research by Boyer and Cohen was made possible by discoveries made two decades earlier by the American biologist James Watson (1928–   ) and the English chemist Francis Crick (1916–2004). In 1953, Watson and Crick announced that genetic information is stored in large, complex molecules known as deoxyribonucleic acid, or *DNA*. They showed how the characteristic arrangement of certain chemical groups, known as base pairs, might provide a mechanism by which genetic information is stored in DNA molecules. Later research showed that the unit of inheritance that had, for more than half a century, been called a gene, was actually nothing more or less than a particular sequence of base pairs in a DNA molecule. The research of Watson, Crick, and their successors has brought about a revolution in the biological sciences in which many of the processes that take place in living organisms are now explained and understood in terms of chemistry. Indeed, the now-familiar phrase *new biology* refers to the fact that much of the research in biology is actually chemical in nature.

The diagram on page 91 shows a segment of a DNA molecule. The molecule consists of two very long strands wrapped around each other in a configuration known as a double helix. The strands consist of alternating sugar and phosphate groups. The sugar present in DNA is deoxyribose. Attached to each phosphate group on each strand is one of four nitrogen bases. The bases are adenine (A), cytosine (C), guanine (G), and thymine (T).

The nitrogen bases are not arranged randomly on the two strands, but always occur in specific base pairs. An adenine always pairs with a thymine (A-T), and a cytosine always pairs with a guanine (C-

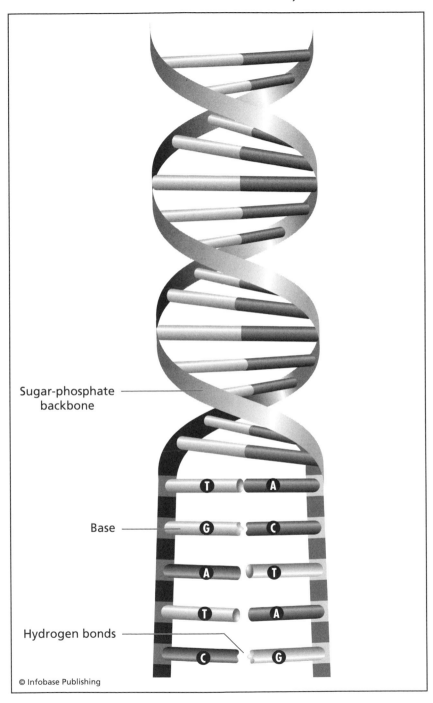

Structure of a DNA molecule

-C-C-T-T-A-G-C-T-G-G-A-A-G-T-C-C-T-A-
-G-G-A-A-T-C-G-A-C-C-T-T-C-A-G-G-A-T-

© Infobase Publishing

Segment of a gene

G). The human genome is thought to contain about 30,000 to 40,000 genes. These genes range in size from a few hundred base pairs to more than 10,000 base pairs. A small segment of a gene might have a structure similar to the diagram above.

Over the last half-century, scientists have learned a great deal about the way in which DNA carries out a variety of essential functions in the cell, such as the production of proteins, and the way in which DNA molecules replicate themselves. They have discovered that organisms have evolved a variety of highly specialized chemical molecules (enzymes) that make possible these functions. One group of these molecules is known as *restriction enzymes* (REs) or *restriction endonucleases.* Restriction enzymes were discovered in the 1960s by the Swiss microbiologist Werner Arber (1929–  ). Arber found that bacteria had evolved a mechanism for protecting themselves from infections by bacteriophages, a type of virus that infects bacteria. He determined that bacteria contain enzymes that are able to recognize distinctive base pair patterns in the DNA of a bacteriophage. When these enzymes locate those base pairs in a strand of DNA, they cut the bonds that hold the base pairs together, essentially destroying the DNA and inactivating the bacteriophage.

Today, many hundreds of REs are known, each designed to scout out characteristic base pair patterns and cut those patterns in a specific location. The chart on page 93 shows some examples of REs, the base pair patterns they recognize, and the point at which they make a cut in the base pair sequence. Notice that some REs cut the two DNA strands at points directly opposite each other forming two segments with *blunt* ends.

# ◁ SOME EXAMPLES OF RESTRICTION ENZYMES ▷

| RESTRICTION ENZYME | BACTERIAL SOURCE | BASE PAIR SEQUENCE RECOGNIZED AND POINT OF STAGGERED CUT* |
|---|---|---|
| EcoRI | Escherichia coli | G\|AATTC<br>CTTAA\|G |
| BamHI | Bacillus amylo-liquefaciens | G\|GATCC<br>CCTAG\|G |
| HindIII | Haemophilus influenzae | A\|AGCTT<br>TTCGA\|A |
| Sau3A1 | Staphylo-coccus aureus | N\|GATC**<br>NCTA\|G |
| TaqI | Thermus aquaticus | T\|CGA<br>AGC\|T |
| **BLUNT CUT** | | |
| AluI | Arthrobacgter luteus | AG\|CT<br>TC\|GA |
| StuI | Streptomyces tubercidicus | AGG\|CCT<br>TCC\|GGA |

*Vertical line (|) represents point of cleavage.
** N represents any base.

The diagram below shows how the enzyme *Alu*I, for example, would cut a DNA segment:

AGG|CCT AGG CCT

→

TCC|GGA TCC GGA

Other REs, however, make staggered cuts, in which the portions cut on each strand are separated from each other by a small number of base pairs. The diagram below shows how the enzyme *Eco*RI makes a staggered cut in a DNA segment:

G|AATTC G AATTC

→

CTTAA|G CTTAA G

The earliest experiments on recombinant DNA (rDNA) were made possible in the early 1970s when Cohen and Boyer discovered that the research they were doing independently had overlapping signifi-

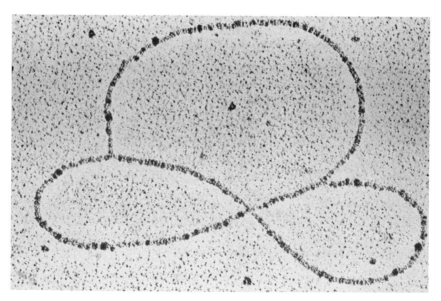

Plasmids are circular pieces of DNA that occur in bacteria and yeast. (NIH/Kakefuda/ Photo Researchers, Inc.)

cance. Cohen, at Stanford University, was investigating the mechanism by which the bacterium *E. coli* could be made to incorporate into its cell a plasmid known as pSC101 that conferred resistance to the antibiotic tetracycline. A plasmid is a circular loop of DNA found in prokaryotic cells, such as bacteria. Boyer, at the University of California at San Francisco, was studying REs. In 1972, the two biochemists began working together to develop methods for inserting modified plasmids created with REs into a variety of organisms.

In their first experiments, Boyer and Cohen worked with the plasmid pSC101 (whose name means that it is a plasmid [*p*] discovered by Stanley Cohen [*SC*] with a specific designation [*101*]. pSC101 is a very simple plasmid containing a gene for replication and a gene that confers resistance to tetracycline. When inserted into another cell, these two genes mean that the plasmid will be able to replicate and that its presence can be detected because the cell will not die when exposed to tetracycline.

In the first step of their initial experiment, as shown in the diagram on page 96, Boyer and Cohen cut the pSC101 plasmid with the restriction enzyme *EcoRI*. The enzyme makes a staggered cut in the plasmid, as shown in the table on page 93. The ends of the cut are said to be "sticky" because they are able to pair with base pairs from *any* strand of DNA with a complementary base pair pattern. A new gene that confers resistance to the antibiotic kanamycin is then mixed with the cleaved plasmid. The kanamycin gene also has been cut by *EcoRI* and has sticky ends that are complementary to those of the cleaved plasmid.

To the mixture of cleaved plasmid and kanamycin gene they added *DNA ligase,* an enzyme that catalyzes the formation of *hydrogen bonds* between two DNA fragments. In other words, the ligase brought about the formation of a "hybrid," or recombinant, DNA molecule that contained DNA from both the original pSC101 plasmid and the kanamycin gene.

In the next step in the experiment, Boyer and Cohen mixed the altered plasmid with a colony of *E. coli* bacteria. In the Boyer-Cohen experiment (and others of its kind), the step was accomplished simply by making a physical mixture of the altered plasmid and the bacteria on a petri dish. Two antibiotics, tetracyclin and kanamycin, were also added to the petri dish. Over time, some of the bacteria on the petri dish absorbed altered plasmids into their cell structures. These bacteria were transformed because they contained not only their own genes but also genes from the plasmid that they had absorbed. Such organisms are sometimes called *chimeras,* after a creature from Greek mythology with the head of a lion, the body of a goat, and the tail of a serpent. They are also called *transgenic* organisms because they contain genes from some other foreign organism.

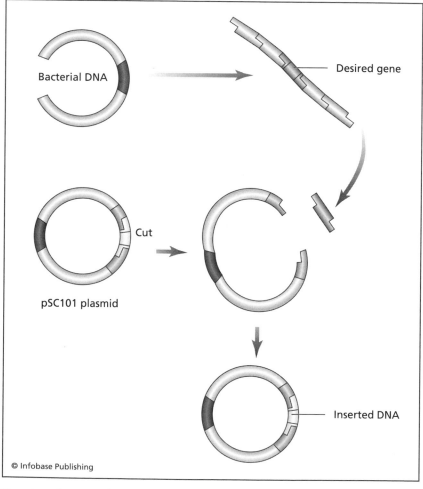

Gene insertion procedure

This sheep-goat chimera was created by combining DNA from each species in an egg that was later implanted into a surrogate mother. (Geoff Tompkinson/Photo Researchers, Inc.)

As the altered bacteria reproduced, later generations carried with them the altered plasmids that provided them with immunity to the two antibiotics on the petri dish. Bacteria that had *not* taken up the altered plasmids had immunity to tetracycline, but not to kanamycin, so they were killed off. Bacteria that *had* taken up the altered plasmids had immunity to both antibiotics and were able to survive and reproduce. When Boyer and Cohen examined the petri dishes containing bacteria and two antibiotics, they found that some colonies were able to survive and reproduce, proving that they had incorporated the altered plasmids into their cell bodies.

Having successfully transferred DNA from one unicellular organism to another unicellular organism, Boyer and Cohen decided to show that their technique was applicable to more complex organisms. They repeated the experiment described above, but used this time a gene from the South African toad, *Xenopus laevis*. That is, the gene was removed from the DNA of *X. laevis* cells and then inserted into *E. coli* cells. To determine whether the bacterial cells incorporated the *X. laevis* DNA, they immobilized frog RNA on a nitrocellulose membrane and then added cell extracts from *E. coli* to the membrane. When cells from altered *E. coli* were used (that is, cells that had incorporated the *X. laevis* gene), the RNA bonded with *E. coli* extracts, while in cells from native *E. coli* (that which had not been altered with an *X. laevis* gene), no bonding was observed.

The transfer of a gene from one organism to another by the Boyer-Cohen technique described above was certainly an intellectual tour-de-force. Yet, the general principles involved were relatively simple and straightforward. Much of the credit due Boyer and Cohen arises from their ability to find ways of carrying out the two or three basic steps involved in producing a recombinant organism: finding ways to cleave a DNA sequence in just the right place;

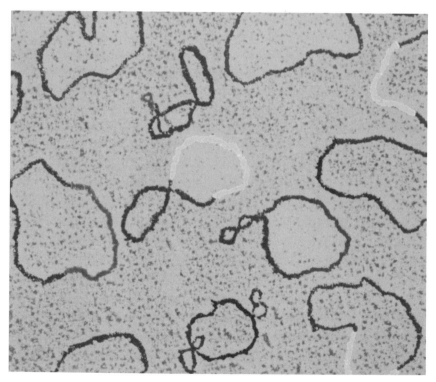

The plasmids in this electron microscope photograph contain segments of DNA that have been inserted into their circular structure. (Dr. Gopal Murti/Photo Researchers, Inc.)

learning how to join the DNA from two organisms (such as a frog and a plasmid); figuring out how to insert the hybrid DNA into the host organism (*E. coli* cells in the above example); and proving that insertion of DNA from one organism into a second organism had, in fact, actually occurred.

## Techniques of Gene Insertion

Over the past three decades, researchers have developed a number of procedures that improve on the basic methodology of Boyer and Cohen. One area in which progress has occurred involves methods for transferring DNA from a donor organism (or DNA prepared synthetically) to a host organism (a process known as *gene insertion*). Those methods can be divided into two general classes: those that use living organisms (called *vectors*) and those that use mechanical methods. The three most common insertion methods using vector organisms employ bacteria, viruses, and yeast artificial chromosome (YAC).

The most common vector used to introduce DNA into plant cells is a bacterium by the name of *Agrobacterium tumefaciens. A. tumefaciens* is a microorganism that lives in the soil and infects plants, causing a disease known as crown gall disease. The bacterium contains a plasmid called the *Ti* (for tumor-inducing) plasmid, which is altered to include the DNA segment to be introduced into a plant. The DNA segment responsible for crown gall disease is also altered, disabling it so that the bacterium is no longer pathogenic when introduced into plant cells.

A second method of gene insertion makes use of viruses. Two common examples are geminiviruses, used to alter the DNA of corn and wheat cells, and caulimoviruses, used to transform members of the mustard family (*Brassicaceae*), which includes Brussels sprouts, cabbage, broccoli, cauliflower, turnip, and a variety of mustards. Viruses are pieces of DNA encased in a protein shell. They serve well as vectors because they are able to attach themselves to a cell's outer surface and inject their DNA into it. Once inside the cell, the viral DNA takes over the cell's machinery and begins making copies of itself, destroying the host cell in the process. To be used as a vector, two changes in the viral DNA (or RNA) are necessary. First, instructions for viral replication must be disabled so that the virus, once inside the cell, is no longer able to replicate itself. Second, the gene to be inserted into the host cell must be added to the viral DNA.

As its name suggests, the third common insertion vector, yeast artificial chromosome (YAC) is a synthetic plasmid-like structure prepared especially for the insertion of genes into organisms. A YAC consists essentially of three parts: a telomere (either end of a eukaryotic chromosome), a centromere (the central part of a chromosome), and a number of restriction sites at which restriction enzymes can cut. The gene (or genes) to be transferred are inserted into a YAC, which is then mixed with host organism cells. Some of these cells incorporate the YACs, forming a transgenic organism. The YACs' property of special interest is their ability to accommodate very large genes. Their maximum capacity is about 1 million base pairs; by contrast, the limit is of about 10,000 base pairs for plasmids and about 25,000 base pairs for most viruses.

A number of non-vector techniques are also available for inserting a gene into a cell. One approach is to create tiny pores in the walls of host cells by some chemical or physical method, openings that allow genes to enter the cell body more easily. These processes are known, respectively, as *chemical poration* and *electroporation* or *laser poration*. In chemical poration, the addition of some chemical to the host cell causes pores to open in the cell membrane, allowing a gene or genes to flow into the cell's interior. Electroporation accomplishes the same result by administering a brief electrical shock, and laser poration does so by exposing host cells to a microscopic laser beam. As with other methods of gene insertion, scientists do not entirely understand the processes by which genes are incorporated into the cell body, and they cannot reliably predict how many will be taken in or the mechanism by which they will eventually be expressed.

Another method of gene insertion is called *bioballistics*, or *biolistics*. Bioballistics makes use of thin metal slivers that are coated with the genes to be inserted and then fired into the host cell by some mechanism. One such mechanism is the *gene gun*, shown in the diagram on page 101. The earliest gene guns looked and

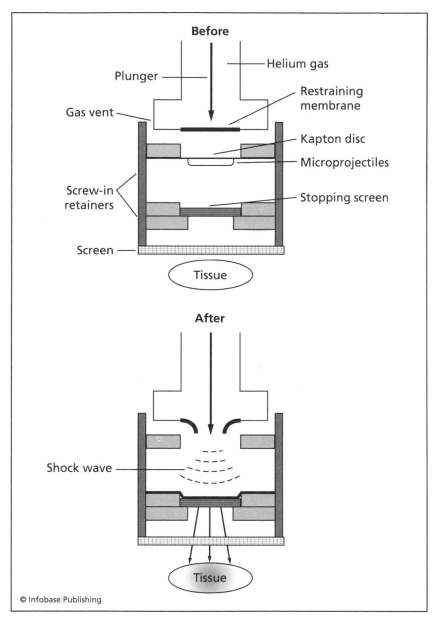

Before

Plunger

Helium gas

Gas vent

Restraining membrane

Kapton disc

Microprojectiles

Screw-in retainers

Stopping screen

Screen

Tissue

After

Shock wave

Tissue

© Infobase Publishing

Design of a gene gun

acted much like other types of guns, using gunpowder charges to fire microscopic coated BBs or pellets into a cell. Such guns were generally too powerful, however, and were unable to insert genes without destroying the target cells. Today's gene guns are more sophisticated, using compressed helium gas to produce a shock wave that fires coated projectiles into a group of cells. These gene guns fire not only metal slivers but also tiny metallic beads, usually made of gold or tungsten; all such projectiles are coated with the genes to be added to the host cell.

A number of variations on the helium-powered gene gun have been developed. They differ from the original gene guns primarily in the mechanism used to accelerate the projectiles into the cell. They use, for instance, centripetal, magnetic, or electrical forces; spray systems; mechanical impulses; shock waves; or electrical discharges.

Finally, for cells that are large enough, genes can be inserted into a cell directly by means of a fine-bore micropipette. The gene to be transferred is first removed from the source with the micropipette. The micropipette is then inserted through the cell membrane of the host cell, and the gene released into the cell body. Under suitable circumstances (which are usually not well understood), the host cell takes up the gene, incorporates it into its own genomic structure, and begins to reproduce it along with its native genes.

## Genetically Modified Products

Recombinant DNA procedures like those described here now have a number of practical applications. One of the most promising is the development of genetically modified (GM) foods and agricultural products, substances whose genetic composition has been altered by rDNA or some similar process. Some examples of genetically modified products are corn plants that have been altered to emit a poison when attacked by pests; tomato plants that spoil at a significantly slower rate than natural plants; rape plants that have been engineered to be resistant to pesticides; and rice that has been enriched with a gene that codes for the production of vitamin A.

One of the first GM agricultural products to be developed was a biological control agent named Frostban. The principle behind

Recombinant DNA procedures are commonly used to introduce pesticide resistance into a crop. (Maximilian Stock Ltd./Photo Researchers, Inc.)

the development of Frostban is that frost does not begin to form on plants in nature, even if the temperature is low enough, in the absence of certain frost-promoting bacteria. Frostban was a spray that contained other types of bacteria that had been genetically modified to destroy the frost-promoting bacteria. When Frostban was sprayed on a crop, these genetically modified bacteria attacked and destroyed frost-promoting bacteria, preventing plants from freezing even when the temperature was low enough for that process to occur normally.

The first field-testing of Frostban in 1986 was met by strong re-action from activists who were concerned about the unknown ef-fects the new product might have on the surrounding environment. On the night before the test spray was to occur, these activists crawled through the field where Frostban was to be tested and pulled up all the strawberry plants on which the test was to occur. In spite of this effort, the spray was eventually tested and found to be effective. It was never produced on a large scale for commercial use, however.

The first GM product to reach the marketplace was a tomato produced by Calgene, Inc., that was given the name of Flavr Savr. The tomato was approved for use by the FDA on May 18, 1994. It was developed to provide consumers with fresher-tasting tomatoes during the winter months, when fresh tomatoes are generally not available. At the time, the only way for people in cold climates to get fresh tomatoes during the winter months was for those tomatoes to be picked while they were still green, allowing them to reach the marketplace before they began to rot.

To solve this problem Calgene scientists synthesized a copy of the gene in tomatoes that causes them to soften over time. That gene normally promotes the production of an enzyme, polygalacturonase, that breaks down cell walls. The scientists then inserted the gene into tomato plants in *reverse* sequence (a process known as *antisense insertion*) so that it would produce an effect opposite that which it normally causes; that is, it inhibited the production of polygalacturonase, causing the tomatoes to soften more slowly than would normally be the case in nature. The advantage of the Flavr Savr tomato was that it could be left on the vine longer, until it had actually ripened, before being picked.

In 1991 Calgene asked the U.S. Food and Drug Administration (FDA) to review the company's research on the Flavr Savr and determine whether it was safe for consumer sales. In May 1994, the FDA agreed that it was. It reported that Flavr Savr was "as safe as tomatoes bred by conventional means" and authorized Calgene to market its new product to the general public.

In spite of FDA's approval, Flavr Savr tomatoes were never a commercial success. Some observers have blamed the product's failure on consumer resistance (because the altered tomatoes cost too much or did not taste good enough). Others claimed that the company did not market the new product correctly or aggressively enough, and still others suggested that complaints about the use of GM products led to the product's downfall. In any case, Calgene was bought out by the chemical giant Monsanto in 1995 and shortly thereafter the parent company ceased research on and production of the Flavr Savr tomato.

A number of other GM foods have, however, met with greater commercial success than either Frostban or Flavr Savr. Some examples are golden rice and various *Bt* foods.

Golden rice is the name given to a genetically modified food that supporters hope will solve vitamin A deficiency (VAD), a widespread health problem in many developing nations. The most serious consequences of VAD are blindness and, in some cases, death. By some estimates, as many as 125 million children worldwide may suffer from VAD.

In the 1990s, the Swiss botanist Ingo Potrykus (1933–  ) developed a possible solution to the problem of VAD. Potrykus and his colleagues at the Institute of Plant Sciences at ETH Zürich (Eidgenössische Technische Hochschule Zürich) developed a modified form of common rice seed that includes three additional genes: *psy* (phytocene synthase), *lcy* (lycopene cyclase), and *crt1* (phytoene desaturase). These genes have critical roles in the synthesis of beta-carotene, a precursor of vitamin A. Golden rice is so named because GM rice containing these three genes has a yellowish color because the *lcy* gene is obtained from the daffodil.

Like other GM food products, golden rice has its share of critics. Some authorities suggest that children for whom golden rice is intended may not be able to digest, absorb, and convert the beta-carotene produced in the product. These children require an adequate, more complete diet that includes sufficient levels of protein and fat if they are to benefit from the engineered product. Some observers suggest that much simpler solutions, such as providing a few teaspoons of red palm oil, readily available in many areas, would provide as much benefit as that provided by golden rice. Proponents argue that no single food product can be expected to meet all the needs of hungry people in developing nations, but that golden rice has many attractive features that can help with at least one major health problem, VAD. (For an extended discussion of the pros and cons of golden rice, see "Golden Rice" at http://www.biotech-info. net/golden.html.)

Bt corn is a genetically modified food named for the organism from which the transmitted gene is taken, the common soil bacterium *Bacillus thuringiensis*. These bacteria produce proteins known

---

# ◄ INGO POTRYKUS (1933– ) ►

One of the most contentious issues in the debate over GM foods has focused on the development of "golden rice," a food product that has been engineered to provide increased levels of vitamin A to those who eat it. Golden rice was developed in the 1990s by Swiss botanist Ingo Potrykus and his colleagues at the Institute of Plant Sciences at ETH Zürich (Eidgenössische Technische Hochschule Zürich). Proponents of golden rice argue it can significantly reduce the problem of blindness and death in up to 250 million children around the world. Opponents say that developers of the product have overestimated its potential benefits and that releasing the engineered product into the environment may have unknown and possibly dangerous effects on human health and the environment.

Ingo Potrykus was born in Hirschberg, Germany, on December 5, 1933. He studied botany, zoology, genetics, biochemistry, philosophy, and physical education at the universities of Cologne and Erlangen and earned his Ph.D. in plant genetics at the Max-Planck-Institute for Plant Breeding Research in Cologne in 1968. He then accepted an appointment at the Institute of Plant Physiology at Hohenheim, where he remained from 1970 to 1974. Potrykus then served as research group leader at the Max-Planck-Institute for Genetics in Ladenburg from 1974 to 1976 and as research group leader at the Friedrich Miescher Institute in Basel, Switzerland, from 1976 to 1986. In the latter year, he was appointed full professor in plant sciences at ETH Zürich.

Potrykus first became interested in the development of transgenic plants in the early 1970s, when he was assistant professor at the Institute

---

as delta endotoxins (or *insecticidal crystal proteins* [ICP]) that are toxic to a wide variety of insects. More than 150 insects belonging to the orders Lepidoptera (such as butterflies and moths), Diptera (flies), and Coleoptera (beetles) are known to be susceptible to the action of Bt delta endotoxins.

The mechanism of this action is now well understood. While intact, the proteins are nontoxic to the insect. When an insect ingests one of these proteins, however, it dissolves in the animal's intestinal fluid. Once the protein has dissolved, enzymes in the insect's guts known as *proteases* attack it. These proteases break the protein

of Plant Physiology at the University of Hohenheim in Stuttgart. "Even at the peak of success of the Green Revolution," Potrykus has written, "it was clear that feeding the exploding population in developing countries would require intensive new scientific research." Potrykus decided that his earlier research on transgenic petunia plants might provide a new line of research that could contribute to a solution of the world's food problems. In that research, Potrykus had successfully transplanted the gene for red color from red petunia plants into white petunia plants, producing "a greenhouse full" of pink plants.

Efforts to replicate the petunia-plant success with food plants proved to be much more difficult, however, and it was not until the late 1980s that Potrykus and his colleagues began to experience success in developing a transgenic form of rice that carried and expressed genes that led to the synthesis of vitamin A, the progenitor of today's golden rice. By the early 21st century, golden rice had become a commercial reality, an accomplishment that Potrykus credited to a number of factors, including "stable, public funding over a long period of time," "substantial financial support from the Rockefeller Foundation," "an enthusiastic group of coworkers (over 60)," and a "naive" belief in the eventual success of the golden rice concept.

Potrykus retired from his position at ETH in 1999. Retirement has not meant retirement from research or interest in genetically modified crops, however. Potrykus continues to write, speak, and carry out his own research on GM foods that, he fervently believes, will someday provide an essential link in the world's solution to problems of hunger and nutrition.

down into smaller units, some of which *are* toxic to the animal. The smaller units formed by the degradation of delta endotoxins bind to the insect's stomach wall and begin to destroy epithelial cells, thus paralyzing its digestive system. The insect stops feeding and may begin to vomit and have diarrhea. After a few hours or a few days of reduced activity and generalized paralysis, the insect dies.

A number of variants of the Bt delta endotoxin are known in nature, each toxic to specific types of insects in the orders Lepidoptera, Diptera, and Coleoptera. Insects against which these endotoxins are effective include alfalfa caterpillar, alfalfa looper, cabbage

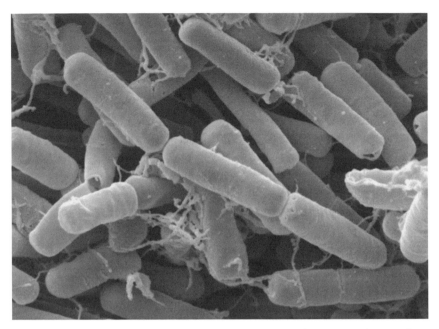

A culture of *Bacillus thuringiensis* culture bacteria. (SciMAT/Photo Researchers, Inc.)

looper, cabbage worm, Colorado potato beetle, diamondback moth, European corn borer, fall webworm, green worm, gypsy moth, hemlock looper, leafrollers, pine budworm, pine butterfly, red-humped caterpillar, spiny elm caterpillar, spruce budworm, tent caterpillars, tomato fruit worm, tobacco hornworm, and tussock moth.

The *Bacillus thuringiensis* bacterium was discovered in 1901 by a Japanese bacteriologist by the name of Shigetane Ishiwatari. Its insecticidal effects were not noted until a decade later, when the German bacteriologist Ernst Berliner observed them. Bt-based insecticides that could be sprayed on plants were first introduced in the 1920s and were first licensed in the United States in 1961. With the growth of recombinant DNA technology in the 1990s, scientists found methods to incorporate *B. thuringiensis* genes directly into plants rather than having the insecticide sprayed on them. Today, several genetically engineered crops containing Bt genes are commercially available for agriculture use, including Bt corn, Bt tomatoes, Bt cotton, and a Bt potato:

➤ Bt corn is sold under the names Maximizer and YieldGard by Novartis and Monsanto, respectively. The product provides resistance to the European corn borer. A third Bt corn, StarLink, produced by Aventis, was withdrawn from the market when some consumers claimed severe allergic reactions to the product and questioned its safety.

➤ Bt tomatoes developed by Monsanto have been approved for human consumption by regulatory agencies in the United States, Canada, and other nations, although they have not yet been made commercially available.

➤ Bt cotton is another genetically modified food produced by Monsanto, resistant to attack by a variety of pests, including the cotton bollworm, tobacco budworm, and the pink bollworm.

➤ Bt potato is produced by Monsanto and marketed under its NewLeaf brand name. In this potato, Bt genes are incorporated that provide resistance to the Colorado potato beetle, a pest that can destroy as much as 85 percent of the potato crop in some areas. The U.S. Environmental Protection Agency (EPA) gave approval for the product in 1995, but it never received a very large share of the market (usually less than 5 percent), and it was withdrawn from use in 2001.

Recombinant DNA techniques have also been used to provide herbicide resistance to a variety of agricultural crops. A leader in this field has again been the Monsanto corporation, which markets the very successful and highly profitable herbicide *Roundup*. The problem with using Roundup, as with other herbicides, is that the product is as likely to kill a cash crop (such as corn or soybeans) as it is to kill the weeds for which it is intended. Monsanto's solution to this problem was to insert a gene into the cash crops that provides resistance to the herbicide. A crop thus modified can be sprayed with Roundup without fear that the herbicide will kill the desired crop as well as weeds.

The active ingredient in Roundup is a compound known as glyphosphate (N-(phosphonomethyl)glycine). Glyphosphate attacks a plant by binding to the active site in an enzyme known as enol-pyruvalshikimate phosphate (ESP) synthase. EPSP synthase has an essential role in the synthesis of certain aromatic amino acids (tyrosine, phenylalanine, and tryptophan). When its EPSP synthase enzyme is inactivated, a plant cannot make essential amino acids or synthesize proteins. It stops growing and eventually dies.

The problem is that glyphosphate acts in essentially the same way on all kinds of plants, both weeds and crops. Someone using the herbicide has to be very careful, then, to make sure that the product is sprayed *only* on weeds and not on crops themselves. (Note that Roundup has no effect on animals since they do not produce tyrosine, phenylalanine, and tryptophan by the mechanism used by plants.)

Monsanto's method of providing herbicide resistance to crop plants has been to introduce a gene that codes for the production of a compound *similar to* EPSP synthase but sufficiently different in molecular structure that glycophosphate will not block it. With this gene, the crop plant can continue to make tyrosine, phenylalanine, and tryptophan and the proteins on which they are based; that is, it can continue to grow and develop normally at the same time that weeds in its vicinity are being killed off by Roundup. Crops that contain the gene for the modified EPSP synthase are marketed by Monsanto under the Roundup Ready label.

The vast majority of GM foods developed so far have been designed to improve agricultural techniques, to provide plants with greater pest and pesticide resistance. However, researchers see a much broader range of applications for recombinant DNA techniques. Some of the most important of these applications are in the field of improving human health. The development of golden rice, described above, is one such development. Another example of the use of genetic engineering to improve the nutritional value of food is the invention in the 1990s of a modified form of canola, a form of rapeseed. Canola and rapeseed are members of the mustard family.

People have grown rapeseed for thousands of years for use as a food and a source of oils for household and industrial purposes. Over a long period of time, a program of selective plant breeding led to the development of a modified form of rapeseed that came to be known as canola. In 1985, the FDA announced that rapeseed and canola were different enough from each other to qualify as separate plant forms. Since that time, researchers have used recombinant DNA procedures to develop a broad range of canola varieties with nutritional properties superior to those of earlier varieties.

For example, in the early 1990s the Calgene company began testing a form of genetically engineered canola high in lauric acid. The high-laurate canola was given the trade name of Laurical. Laurical has most of the desirable nutritional properties of tropical oils, such as coconut and palm oil, with better shelf life and a silky texture that makes it highly desirable for use in confectionery products. In other words, the engineered oil was, overall, healthier and commercially more attractive than any existing natural product.

Another way that GM foods may improve human health is through the development of *edible vaccines*. An edible vaccine is a vaccine produced when one or more genes for an antigen are added to some natural food, such as potatoes or bananas. When a person eats that food, he or she ingests the antigen, which may provide immunity to a given disease.

Transgenic plants are also being considered for a number of industrial applications. For example, researchers are attempting to design and breed genetically modified plants to produce biofuels that are less harmful to the environment than traditional fossil fuels. Engineered plants may be developed that yield biolubricants to replace traditional hydraulic fluids or that produce biodegradable plastics with specially designed physical and chemical properties.

Since the first appearance of commercial GM crops in the 1990s, their popularity among farmers in the United States has exploded. Between 1996 and 2002, the amount of farmland devoted to the growth of GM crops has increased by 3,000 percent in the United States. The new agricultural technology has been far less successful in other parts of the world, however. As of 2004, six countries accounted for 99 percent of all the GM crops grown in the world. The United States led the way with 63 percent of all GM cropland, followed by Argentina (20 percent), Canada (6 percent), Brazil (5 percent), China (4 percent), and South Africa (1 percent). According to some estimates, about 70 percent of all the food products currently available to American consumers contain one or more GM products.

The most widely grown engineered food is GM soybeans, which account for 63 percent of all the cropland devoted to engineered crops in the United States, followed by GM corn (19 percent), GM cotton (13 percent), and GM canola (5 percent). The table below shows the percentage of three crops grown in the United States in 2002–2003 that consisted of modified plants. The major characteristics for which modified plants in the United States have been developed are herbicide tolerance and insect resistance. The circle graph accompanying the following table shows the plant characteristics for which GM foods in the United States have been tested as of 2003.

The year 2006 marked the end of the first decade during which genetically modified crops were available in the United States. Studies of agricultural changes during that decade produced mixed findings. On the one hand, many farmers had enthusiastically adopted GM crops, corn, soybeans, and cotton in particular. The main reasons

## ◁ PERCENT OF ALL FARMLAND DEVOTED TO GM CROPS IN THE UNITED STATES (2003) ▷

| CROP | INSECT-RESISTANT VARIETIES (BT) | | HERBICIDE-RESISTANT VARIETIES | |
|---|---|---|---|---|
| | 2002 | 2003 | 2002 | 2003 |
| corn | 22 | 26 | 9 | 9 |
| cotton | 13 | 16 | 36 | 30 |
| soybeans | 75 | 80 | 75 | 80 |

Source: National Agricultural Statistics Service.

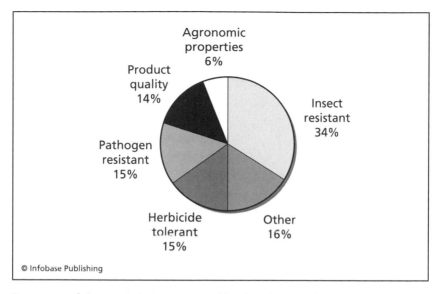

Percentage of characteristics in engineered foods in the United States in 2002–03

for their decisions were expectations of higher yields, savings in management time, and lower pesticide costs. As a result, nearly 100 percent of the soybeans planted in the United States in 2006 came from GM seeds and about half of all the cotton planted had also been genetically engineered. Still, GM crops caused concern among the general public, with a number of groups calling for a halt to further planting of GM seeds. These demands were especially pronounced in the European Union, where a number of nations had by 2006 passed legislation to prohibit the planting, sale, or transport of modified foods.

## Controversy about GM Foods

The development of genetically modified food products has created a certain amount of controversy in the United States, the European Union, and other parts of the world. The level of controversy, however, differs substantially. According to a poll published by the Pew Research Center in late 2003, for example, about a third of all

This farmer is growing a genetically modified form of barley. (Chris Knapton/Photo Researchers, Inc.)

Americans said that they know "a great deal" or "some" information about GM foods, a 10 percent decline from a 2001 poll on the same subject. Opposition to the introduction of GM foods into the American food supply also dropped during the same period, from 58 percent in 2001 to 48 percent in 2003. However, that opposition tends to be strong among a certain minority of the population, with a slight decrease from 35 percent in 2001 to 31 percent in 2003.

A similar Pew study conducted in 2003 of attitudes about GM foods in seven nations (Canada, France, Germany, Great Britain, Italy, Japan, and the United States) found strikingly different—and more negative—results. Nearly 9 out of 10 of those interviewed in France, for example, say that genetically altered fruits and vegetables are "bad." Comparable results for the other six nations are shown in the chart on page 115.

Critics have a range of objections to the genetically modified foods. The fundamental problem posed by these objections, however, is the variety of GM products now available: A host of GM products have

| ◁ **ATTITUDES ABOUT GENETICALLY ALTERED FOODS IN SEVEN NATIONS, 2003** ▷ | | | |
|---|---|---|---|
| **NATION** | **OPINION REGARDING SCIENTIFICALLY ALTERED FRUITS AND VEGETABLES** | | |
| | **GOOD (%)** | **BAD (%)** | **NO OPINION (%)** |
| United States | 37 | 55 | 8 |
| Canada | 31 | 63 | 6 |
| Great Britain | 27 | 65 | 8 |
| Japan | 20 | 76 | 4 |
| Italy | 17 | 74 | 9 |
| Germany | 17 | 81 | 2 |
| France | 10 | 89 | 1 |

Source: Pew Research Center for the People and the Press, "Broad Opposition to Genetically Modified Foods."

been developed with a wide range of characteristics. It is difficult to generalize about the threats posed by GM foods when there are so many of them and they are so different from each other. It is *not* possible to say that *all* genetically altered foods are inherently harmful to the environment or to human health in some way or another. In fact, it is very difficult to pinpoint specific examples of ways in which any *specific* GM food is a risk to either human health or the environment. There are simply no scientific studies that support such concerns about any GM agricultural product currently available to farmers or consumers.

Some critics of GM foods have a more general concern about altering natural products. They feel there is something inherently wrong with efforts to change the composition of natural foods by recombinant DNA or other "artificial" procedures, even if it cannot be demonstrated scientifically. The occurrence of food-borne diseases unrelated to genetic engineering of foods has heightened such concerns. The outbreak of bovine spongiform encephalopathy (more commonly known as BSE or mad cow disease) in the United Kingdom in the late 1980s engendered a generalized concern about food safety in the European Union for well over a decade. People who may never have thought very seriously about food safety before the BSE episode began to think more carefully about how their foods were being grown and raised and what steps should be taken to increase food safety for the general public. In this regard, it is hardly surprising that Europeans, who were most at risk during the BSE epidemic, are relatively more suspicious of the possible risks posed by GM foods.

In spite of the uncertainties surrounding GM foods, observers have raised some legitimate scientific concerns about the risks they may pose to human health or the environment. Human health risks of GM foods relate to allergens, toxins, and inadvertent gene transfer to people. Possible environmental risks are that stray genes will form "superseeds," that insect pests will develop resistance to modified plants, and that modified plants will harm unintended species.

## Risks to Human Health

A small proportion of the population is allergic to one or more food products. Some of the most common allergies are to cow's milk, eggs, soybeans, wheat, peanuts, and various tree nuts. Allergic reactions to foods range from very mild to severe. In the most serious cases, a person exposed to an allergen has difficulty breathing, swelling in the mouth and throat, and decreased blood pressure, conditions that can lead to anaphylactic shock and even death.

A potential problem arises, then, if a gene from a potential allergen-containing plant is transferred into a food plant. For example, in the early 1990s, Pioneer Hi-Bred International, Inc., a DuPont subsidiary, developed a transgenic soybean that contained a gene taken from the Brazil nut (*Bertholletia excelsa*). The gene transfer was intended to create a soybean containing more of the amino acid methionine, an essential nutrient in which soybeans are normally deficient. It did so, but studies at the University of Nebraska showed that it also conferred the allergenic characteristics of the Brazil nut, making the transgenic soybean itself allergenic. People with food allergies learn early to adjust their diet so as to avoid exposure to allergenic foods. But a person allergic to Brazil nuts might feel safe eating a soybean product, not realizing its allergenic potential. When informed of the results of the Nebraska study, Pioneer discontinued its research on the Brazil nut–enhanced soybean. The case illustrates the potential, however, of the transfer of allergens during genetic transformations.

Perhaps one of the best-known problems associated with the possible appearance of allergens in modified foods involved a product known as StarLink corn, developed by Aventis CropScience in the 1990s. StarLink corn was engineered to include a gene for the synthesis of an insecticidal protein called Cry9C, originally isolated from a strain of the bacterium *B. thuringiensis tolworthi*. The engineered plant was designed to be resistant to two major pests, the European corn borer and the southwestern corn borer, and possibly also to the black cutworm. StarLink was approved for use in the United States as an animal feed and for industrial applications, but not for human consumption.

In September 2000, DNA fragments from Cry9C were detected in taco shells being sold for human consumption. The amount of the engineered protein was very small, estimated to be less than 0.01 percent by weight, the lowest level of test sensitivity. But Aventis and others were concerned that the protein might cause allergic reactions in people who ate the engineered corn. Within a matter of days, Aventis announced that it would no longer authorize the sale of StarLink corn for the 2001 season, and food stores announced a *recall* of taco and other corn products that might contain the engineered corn.

At the same time, various regulatory agencies in the United States began a review of possible health risks from exposure to StarLink corn. By mid-2001, three of the most important agencies had issued statements and reports generally favorable to Aventis. On October 12, 2000, the Environmental Protection Agency stated, the "EPA does not have any evidence that food containing StarLink corn will cause any allergic reaction in people, and the agency believes the risks, if any, are extremely low." Two months later, a special Scientific Advisory Panel released an "Assessment of Scientific Information Concerning StarLink Corn" to the EPA that found "a low probability of allergenicity in the exposed population." Finally, in June 2001, the Centers for Disease Control and Prevention (CDC) delivered its study to the FDA, which focused especially on individuals who reported that they had developed allergic reactions as result of eating products containing StarLink corn. Although these people had suffered allergic reactions, the CDC panel concluded that StarLink was not the cause: "These findings do not provide any evidence that the reactions that the affected people experienced were associated with hypersensitivity to the Cry9c protein." In spite of this generally favorable response, Aventis withdrew StarLink corn from commercial use in October 2000.

Toxins are a second source of concern about the possible health effects of GM foods. Plants have evolved an amazing array of toxins known as *phytotoxins* to resist attacks by predators ranging from bacteria, fungi, insects, and herbivores to human beings. For example, the potato plant produces glycoalkaloid toxins. The glycoalkaloids are a family of complex organic compounds that contain sugars, alkaloids (heterocyclic compounds containing nitrogen), and other organic groups. The glycoalkaloids cause a number of human health problems; they can depress the central nervous system, cause cancer, and inflame the kidneys. Two types of glycoalkaloids commonly found in plants are the solanines and the chaconines, whose structural formulas are shown on page 119.

Since the glycoalkaloids are destroyed by heating and are toxic in only rather large concentrations, they usually do not endanger human health. However, some critics of genetically altered foods point out that gene transfer might inadvertently deliver a phytotoxin gene into a food plant, putting human health at risk. Thus far there appears to be no example of such an event having occurred.

CH₃OH

Chemical structures of α-solanine and α-chaconine

As discussed earlier in this chapter, recombinant DNA techniques can be used to confer resistance to certain antibiotics (such
as tetracyclin and kanamycin) to a host organism. This step in the
recombinant process is a common one because it is an easy way for

researchers to find out which organisms in a study have actually incorporated the gene to be transferred. But the practice could conceivably threaten human health. For example, suppose that a food engineered to contain a gene conferring some desirable characteristic (such as an increased level of some nutrient) also contained a gene for antibiotic resistance. If a person ate the GM food and later found it necessary to take the corresponding antibiotic to treat an illness, what would happen? One might expect that the antibiotic would be destroyed by the gene, and that the person would receive no benefit from the medication. Again, no studies exist confirming that such effects have actually occurred as a result of eating GM foods. Given how difficult it would be to detect such effects, however, it is not entirely surprising that some people worry that unwanted antibiotic resistance will spread to the human population in this manner.

As is apparent from the preceding discussion, a fair number of concerns about the possible effects of GM food on human health have been expressed both by scientists and nonscientists. Although one cannot dismiss the possibility that these effects, or others not yet imagined, could happen, scientific support for such concerns is relatively thin. A report by Jose L. Domingo, of the faculty of Medicine and Health Sciences at Spain's Rovira i Virgili University, underscores this point. Domingo undertook an extensive survey of scientific research on the adverse effects of GM foods that had been conducted as of 2000. Of the 212 reports he reviewed, only seven cited the results of scientific studies on this question. The remaining articles, he discovered, contained comments, opinions, viewpoints, and other observations about GM food without any supporting scientific evidence.

## Environmental Effects

One of the most commonly expressed concerns about possible environmental effects of GM foods is that genes inserted into a modified plant might escape into the surrounding environment and be taken up by wild relatives of the engineered crop plant. Such a possibility exists, some experts say, because of the close taxonomic relationship among some crops plants and weedy relatives. Sunflowers, sorghum, canola, and squash are commonly cited examples of crop plants that have weedy relatives capable of cross-breeding with them. If such interbreeding did happen, weeds would develop the same resistance to herbicides that had been bred into the crop plant, resulting in "superweeds" that might make control efforts even more difficult than they are now. A possible consequence of such gene transfers is that farmers would have to use even stronger pesticides—and more of them—than they use today, increasing the overall risk to the environment.

A study conducted by the environmental group English Nature in late 2001 bears out this risk. The group's research showed that herbicide-resistant genes inserted into certain rapeseed oil crops in Canada had escaped into surrounding areas, resulting in the growth of weeds that also contained the genes. According to Brian Johnson, the organization's adviser for biotechnology, the consequences of using modified seeds could be "that volunteer crops would be harder to control and [farmers] might have to use different, and more environmentally damaging, herbicides to control them."

Chemical companies that have developed such products present different views. For example, representatives from the German chemical company AgrEvo (Hoechst Schering AgrEvo GmbH) have said, for example, that pollen from engineered plants is unlikely to spread more than about 30 feet (10 m) from the parent plant. If gene transmission does occur, they say, the weeds affected will not become superweeds but will inherit a resistance to only a single herbicide, the one for which the engineered crop plant was developed. Besides, they argue, such events do not really change the problem facing farmers, since weeds need to be controlled anyway, no matter how that control is achieved.

One of the strongest arguments for the use of GM foods is that they may lead to substantial reductions in the amount of pesticides used in agriculture. If a gene can be inserted into a crop plant that is lethal to some pest, then a pesticide does not need to be sprayed on that crop. And the overuse of pesticides in agriculture throughout the world has long been one of the most serious concerns among environmentalists about the way in which crops are grown today. A study reported by Australia's Commonwealth Scientific and Industrial Research Organization (CSIRO) in August 2003, for example, showed that cotton farmers in that country had been able to reduce their use of pesticides by 50 percent through the use of a bioengineered cotton called Bollgard II, developed by Monsanto. Bollgard II was designed to provide resistance to some of the most serious pests that attack cotton crops, including bollworms, armyworms, and loopers.

Critics of GM foods are not convinced by this argument. They point out that the use of an engineered pesticide, such as Bollgard II, eventually results in the rise of new members of a pest population that are stronger and more resistant to the pesticide being used. As a result, larger amounts of the pesticide are needed to keep the pest under control during each growing season. Proponents of GM pest control counter that this pattern is true *any time* a pesticide is used, whether it is sprayed on a plant or engineered into the plant's genome. With genetic engineering, at least other risks of pesticide use (such as the risks to workers who have to handle and dispense the chemical) are reduced or eliminated.

In the controversy over GM foods, a handful of research studies have been published that have raised significant concerns about such foods and aroused widespread public opposition to the engineering of foods. One such study was reported in 1999 by a team of researchers from Cornell University led by John Losey. Losey's team fed monarch butterfly caterpillars the leaves of a milkweed plant that had been dusted with pollen from an engineered corn developed by the Swiss chemical company Novartis. Researchers found that nearly half of the caterpillars died and those that did survive did not develop properly. Almost as soon as the study was published in the prestigious English scientific journal *Nature,* both consumer groups and scientists not involved in the study began to denounce GM plants. Two of the United Kingdom's largest supermarket chains, Sainsbury's and Iceland, announced that they were removing all GM foods from their shelves.

Other scientists quickly criticized this knee-jerk reaction. They pointed out that Losey's study provided only preliminary information and that, by comparison, far more monarch butterflies are killed by truck traffic in agricultural areas and as a result of habitat destruction in Mexico than would be destroyed by engineered corn. In November 2000 at a conference in Chicago, entomologists met to analyze the research on engineered corn and monarch butterflies in more detail. They came to the general conclusion that there was no significant difference in the survival rates of monarch butterflies in areas where GM corn had been planted and where it was absent. As one attendee noted, "If there are any differences, they are not very profound." Another study reported by researchers at the University of Maryland concluded that monarch butterflies actually have a much better survival rate in the presence of GM crops than in the presence of crops that have been sprayed with pesticide.

Thus far, the question of possible environmental effects from the use of GM crops has not been resolved. Reasonable arguments to worry about such effects have been set forward. But thus far little scientific evidence is available to support such concerns.

Micropropagation. Cereal plants being grown in test tubes from tissue cultures. (Rosenfeld Images Ltd./Photo Researchers, Inc.)

## Regulatory Issues

The longstanding, often contentious, debate over genetically engineered foods has led to a parallel dispute over whether such foods should be regulated, licensed, or otherwise controlled by governmental agencies. That dispute has been resolved in two quite different ways in the United States and Europe. In this country, the federal government has taken the position that GM foods must meet the same standards of safety that apply to other foods. First, experimental plantings of engineered seeds must be approved by the Animal and Plant Health Inspection Service (APHIS) of the U.S. Department of Agriculture and, if federal funds are involved in the project, by the National Institutes of Health Recombinant DNA Advisory Committee (NIH-RAC). Then the products of such research must be approved by the U.S. Food and Drug Administration (if they are intended for human consumption), by APHIS (if they are designed for purposes other than human consumption), and by the U.S. Environmental Protection Agency (if there is any possibility that the products may result in the release of pollutants to the environment). Once a GM food product has passed those regulatory hurdles, it may be sold to farmers, marketed to consumers, made available to industry, or offered for sale in any other way with no further restrictions or labeling required. In fact, the only effort in the United States to require labeling of GM foods was an initiative referendum held in the State of Oregon in 2002; Measure 27 proposed requiring any food containing GM products made available to Oregon consumer to be so labeled. Voters rejected the proposal by a vote of 73 percent to 27 percent.

The situation in Europe has been very different. As early as April 1990, the parliament of the European Union (EU) began to adopt regulations to be used in the approval of GM foods. Over the next decade, EU states approved nine discrete GM food products under the provisions of those decisions. By 1997, however, a number of member states of the EU had changed course and began to ban the sale of GM foods, including those that had already been approved in 1990. The bans were motivated to some extent by a philosophical concept sometimes known as the *precautionary principle.* The precautionary principle says that governmental agencies may be justified in taking regulatory action even when some scientific uncertainty remains about the possible risks and consequences of a practice. For example, many people today believe that it is appropriate to take action to reduce carbon dioxide emissions by humans because of the possible disastrous environmental consequences of burning fossil fuels. Many European governments and agencies have argued that the precautionary principle should be invoked in the case of GM foods: Even though their health and environmental consequences are not known for certain, those consequences could be serious enough that people should move slowly in developing and using those products.

By June of 1999, environmental ministers of the EU had established an informal, de facto ban on GM foods based on this philosophy. That agreement prohibited both the planting of new GM crops within the European states and the import of GM foods for at least four years.

The EU's action outraged the United States. The United States argued that the decision to ban the import of GM foods was a violation of free-trade agreements between the United States and the European Union. Those agreements, U.S. representatives claimed, prohibited bans by any nation on the free flow of products between countries. In early 2003 the Bush administration filed a formal complaint against EU practices with the World Trade Organization (WTO). It was joined in this action by 12 other nations; Argentina, Canada, Egypt, Australia, New Zealand, Mexico, Chile, Colombia, El Salvador, Honduras, Peru, and Uruguay.

By the time the WTO complaints were lodged, however, the EU had already been rethinking its position on GM foods. A March 2000 decision by the EU's highest judicial body, the European Court of Justice, played a role. According to the court's ruling, France did not have the right to ban three GM crops that had already been approved by the EU in 1990. Gradually, member states began to adopt the position that GM foods could be grown and imported *provided* that they met very strict labeling and traceability standards. These standards were ultimately enshrined in Directive 2001/18/EC, which, among other things, stated (1) that all foods containing more than 0.9 percent genetically modified organisms (GMOs) must be so labeled, and

(2) that all GM foods must contain *traceability tags*. A traceability tag used in GM foods is a piece of DNA that has no effect on human health, the environment, or the organism into which it is inserted, but that provides an "address" of the company that made the product. The traceability tag allows a governmental agency to track down the manufacturer of some food product if it is discovered to have some deleterious effect on human health or the environment.

In May 2004 the ban on GM food in the European Union officially came to an end with approval by the European Commission of a GM corn made by the Swiss company Syngenta. In 2006, the EU set

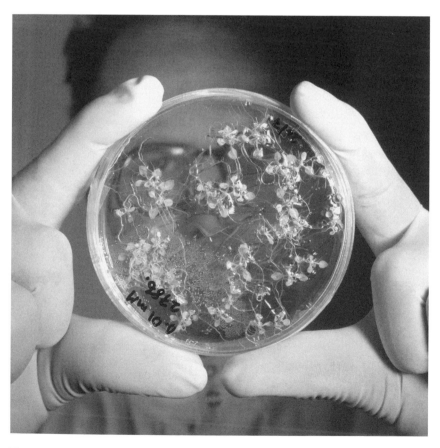

These genetically modified seedlings contain DNA "tags" that make it possible to trace their producer. (Simon Fraser/Photo Researchers, Inc.)

standards for the acceptance of GM foods that included two requirements. First, each product submitted for approval had to be shown to be safe for humans, other animals, and the environment. Second, every product had to be available on a "freedom of choice" basis. That is, every farmer and consumer was to have complete freedom in deciding whether or not to use a GM crop or food. Manufacturers were required to provide data needed to allow people to make those decisions.

Genetically modified crops and foods remain a subject of dispute in most parts of the world. Many farmers and consumers see these products as a valuable addition to the world's food supply. Critics continue to worry that such products may pose problems for the health of humans and other animals and be a threat to the environment.

# 5

# FOOD-BORNE ILLNESSES AND IRRADIATION OF FOODS

Officials at the Colorado Department of Public Health and Environment were concerned. During the first week of August 1997, the agency had received an unusually large number of reports of people who had become ill after eating ground beef. Department researchers had been able to confirm that five of them had eaten ground beef produced by a company called Hudson Foods, a subsidiary of Tyson Foods Inc. The Colorado health department contacted the U.S. Department of Agriculture (USDA) and recommended that it inspect Hudson's beef-processing facility at Columbus, Nebraska.

The USDA's inspection produced troubling results. It suggested that workers at the Columbus plant had used unsanitary procedures in handling beef during the month of June, with the result that ground beef containing *E. coli* bacteria was released to consumers in a number of states. *E. coli* are bacteria that normally live in the intestines of humans and other animals. Most strains of the bacteria are harmless and, indeed, are needed to maintain normal digestive functions. Some strains of the bacteria, however, produce toxins that can result in a variety of disorders, including diarrhea and kidney damage. One of the most common of these strains is *E. coli 0157: H7.* USDA researchers concluded that at least some of the problems reported in Colorado were caused by the presence of *E. coli 0157: H7* bacteria in ground beef from Hudson's Columbus processing plant.

Based on this information, the USDA asked Hudson Foods to close the Columbus plant temporarily, to destroy all beef products at the facility, and to issue recall notices on all ground beef products shipped from the Columbus plant. (In the United States, the USDA can inspect food-processing facilities, but it has no authority to take action on closing facilities or recalling products from contaminated plants.) Eventually, Hudson requested fast-food restaurants, grocery stores, and the like to destroy or return more than 25 million pounds of ground beef supplied to retailers from the Columbus plant.

By the end of August 1997, the USDA concluded that beef from Hudson's Columbus plant had been responsible for fewer than 20 cases of *E. coli* infection, none of which had been fatal. Although the volume of food product destroyed and recalled (more than 25 million pounds) was large, the amount of contaminated food was relatively small, accounting for less than 1 percent of the 8 billion pounds of beef processed in the United States every year.

Nor was the Hudson episode the worst case of food-borne illness in the United States in recent years. The worst recorded case of *E. coli food poisoning* occurred in 1993 when about 700 patrons of the Jack-in-the-Box restaurant chain in Washington State became ill from eating contaminated ground beef. Of that number, four individuals died. In 1999, two other large outbreaks of food poisoning were reported, one in Illinois and one in New York State. In each case, large numbers of people ate food contaminated with *E. coli*. At an event called "Cornstock" in Petersburg, Illinois, more than 200 people were treated at 20 area hospitals, while 751 cases of confirmed and suspected cases of *E. coli* poisoning were reported at New York State's Washington County Fair in September 1999.

## Food-Borne Diseases and Their Prevention

Food-borne illnesses have afflicted humans for centuries, if not for millennia. Historical records suggest, for example, that Antonius Musa, physician to the first Roman emperor, Augustus (63 B.C.E.–14

## ◄ THOMAS WILLIS (1621–1675) ►

*If I have seen further it is by standing
on the shoulders of Giants.*

That quotation, credited to Sir Isaac Newton, reflects the understanding of many great geniuses: that most great accomplishments in science (and in other fields) depend to a large extent on the work of those who have gone before. Sometimes, the early pioneers are themselves famous. At other times, their names are virtually unknown to the general public and, in many cases, even to professionals in the field. Such is arguably the case of one of the great biologists of the 17th century, Thomas Willis.

Willis was born in Great Bedwyn, Wiltshire, England, on January 27, 1621. His father was steward of the manor of Great Bedwyn, and young Thomas received an education typical of that available to working-class youths of the day. He attended Oxford University, from which he earned a bachelor's degree in 1637, a master's in 1639, a second master's in 1642, and his license to practice medicine in 1646. When Willis entered Oxford, he had intended to enter the ministry, but the English Civil War (1642–51), then in progress, made him change his mind. Since he sided with the Royalists, he decided to avoid any controversies that might arise over a career in the church, and he settled on a career in medicine instead. Those same Royalist preferences stood him in good stead when Charles II was restored to the throne in 1660, and he rapidly became a very popular physician in London with a wealthy and influential following.

C.E.), treated his patient for typhoid fever by immersing him in cold water. Credit for the first clinical description of the disease usually goes to the English physician Thomas Willis (1621–75), who in 1659 reported on its symptoms and effects. A clear understanding of the etiology (origin) of the disease was not available, however, for another two centuries. Then, in 1819, the French physician Pierre Fidèle Bretonneau (1778–1862) suggested a mechanism by which the disease is transmitted. Bretonneau incorporated into this description his own primitive germ theory of disease that was later elabo-

Willis had knowledge and experience from a variety of disciplines—including anatomy, physiology, pharmacology, and chemistry—and he brought them to bear on medical problems. He developed keen insight on a number of basic issues in the field. In 1664, for example, he published perhaps his most famous book, *Cerebri anatome* (*Anatomy of the Brain*), which served for some time as physicians' basic text on the anatomy of the central nervous system. In this book, Willis first described a region of the brain in which the basilar and the internal carotid arteries terminate, now called the Circle of Willis.

Willis also provided the first modern definition of typhoid fever, myasthenia gravis, and childbed fever, latter renamed puerperal fever at Willis's suggestion. In each case he furnished careful and detailed descriptions of the signs and symptoms, duration and severity of the disease, the nature of relapses, and recommended methods of treatment. He also rediscovered the relationship between diabetes and sugar in the urine, information known to the ancient Greeks but since forgotten. Willis also expanded knowledge on diabetes, pointing out that the disease occurs in a variety of forms, the most dangerous of which is diabetes mellitus.

In addition to his medical practice in London, Willis held the post of Sedlerian Professor of Natural Philosophy at Oxford from 1660 to 1675 and gave private instruction in the fields of anatomy, medicine, and chemistry. Willis was a member of many important social and professional organizations, including the Philosophical Club of Oxford (precursor to the Royal Society), the Royal Society, and the Royal College of Physicians. He died of pneumonia on November 11, 1675, in London and was buried in Westminister Abbey.

rated and expanded by Louis Pasteur (1822–95), who is usually given credit for "discovery" of the theory.

Scientists now know of at least 200 different food-borne illnesses, the vast majority of which are caused by biological agents (pathogens) such as viruses, bacteria, parasites, prions, or protozoans. Other food-borne illnesses are caused by chemical agents, such as heavy metals or toxins, and still others by physical agents, such as pieces of bone or metal. The table on page 132 lists some typical examples of food-borne illnesses.

## ◄ SOME COMMON FOOD-BORNE ILLNESSES ►

| ILLNESS | AGENT |
| --- | --- |
| salmonella infections | Any of more than 2,000 bacteria belonging to the genus *Salmonella* |
| cholera | *Vibrio cholerae* (bacterium) |
| listerosis | *Listeria monocytogenes* (bacterium) |
| botulism | *Clostridium botulinum* (bacterium) |
| giardiasis | *Giardia lamblia* (parasitic protozoan) |
| trichinosis | *Trichinella spiralis* (a worm belonging to the family Trichinellidae) |
| hepatitis A | hepatitis A virus |
| scombroid (histamine) | chemical toxin produced in some types of seafood poisoning |

Scientists have also learned a great deal about the etiology of food-borne illnesses, the mechanisms by which they are transmitted, and the ways they can be prevented and treated. Such illnesses fall into two general categories, those that result from *food intoxication* (also known as food poisoning) and those caused by *food infection*. Food intoxication describes circumstances in which bacteria release toxins (poisonous materials) into foods. When a person eats the contaminated food, the toxins cause a variety of symptoms that, in the most extreme cases, may result in the person's death. Two of the most common examples of food intoxication are those caused by the bacteria *Staphylococcus* and *Clostridium botulinum.* The illnesses these bacterial toxins cause are known as staphylococcis (or simply staph) infections and botulism, respectively. An important characteristic of food intoxication is that an illness may continue even after the bacteria that cause it have died. Since it is the toxins produced by the bacteria, and not the bacteria themselves, that cause an illness, symptoms may continue even though no bacteria remain in the body.

By contrast with food intoxications, food infections are actually caused by bacteria and other microorganisms that invade the digestive tract and colonize the intestinal epithelium. The microorganisms cause symptoms not only as a result of their own reproduction, but also because they may invade and destroy cells or produce toxins that destroy the host cells. Among the most common food infections are those caused by *Salmonella,* a family of bacteria. One member of that family, *Salmonella typhi,* is responsible for typhoid fever. Another, *S. enteritidis,* is now well known as the agent responsible for outbreaks of salmonella that first appeared widely in the 1980s; many of these outbreaks appear to have been caused by the ingestion of uncooked or inadequately cooked eggs (used, for instance, to make homemade mayonnaise). Scientists discovered that the *S. enteritidis* bacterium had become adapted to living in the ovary of chickens so that eggs produced by infected chickens carried the disease-causing bacterium.

Food can act in one of two quite different ways in the development of a food-borne illness. In some cases, the food serves simply as the medium by which a disease-causing agent (such as a virus or a protozoan) enters the digestive system. The pathogen does not require the food itself for its own survival and reproduction, and simply uses the food as a way of getting into a person's body. Once present in the body, the disease-causing agent begins to grow, reproduce, release toxins, and cause damage to its human or animal host in some other way. In other instances, the food on which the agent travels also provides the nutrients the pathogen needs to survive and reproduce. Bacterial infections are of this type. Once a bacterium has come into contact with a food, it uses that food for its own growth and development, ultimately resulting in either a food intoxication or food infection.

# Trends in Food-Borne Illnesses in the United States

In 1999, the Centers for Disease Control and Prevention (CDC) sponsored an extensive study of the number and types of food-borne illnesses and death occurring annually in the United States (Paul S. Mead, et al., "Food-Related Illness and Death in the United States," *Emerging Infectious Diseases,* September–October 1999, 607–617; since 1999 the CDC has conducted more limited studies of food-borne illnesses in a sample of 10 states only). The study's authors concluded that there are about 76 million cases of food-borne illness each year in the United States, of which about 325,000 require hospitalization and 5,000 result in death. Less than half of all cases of food-borne illness (about 14 million cases) can be associated with known pathogens. Of cases in which a pathogen has been identified, three bacteria—*Salmonella, Listeria,* and *Toxoplasma*—account for 1,500 deaths per year, more than three-quarters of those for which a known pathogen is responsible. Remarkably, a large number of illnesses (62 million), hospitalizations (265,000), and deaths (3,200) are caused by pathogens that have not been identified. Authors of the study concluded, "Overall, food-borne diseases appear to cause more illnesses but fewer deaths than previously estimated." The table on pages 135–138 summarizes a few of the most common pathogens responsible for food-borne illnesses in the United States, and the number of illnesses, hospitalizations, and death caused by each, as reported by the Mead study.

Food-borne illnesses are now closely monitored and studied by various agencies of the federal and state governments. When an outbreak of a food-borne illness occurs, health workers are required to report the event and its characteristics to state and/or federal health agencies. Health officials attempt to collect as much information as possible about each outbreak, including the location of the event, the

# ◁ ESTIMATED FREQUENCIES OF ILLNESSES, HOSPITALIZATIONS, AND DEATHS OF CERTAIN FOOD-BORNE PATHOGENS IN THE UNITED STATES ▷

| AGENT | ILLNESSES | | HOSPITALIZATIONS | | DEATHS | |
| --- | --- | --- | --- | --- | --- | --- |
| | TOTAL | PERCENT* | TOTAL | PERCENT* | TOTAL | PERCENT* |
| Bacterial | | | | | | |
| *Bacillus cereus* | 27,360 | 0.2 | 8 | 0.0 | 0.0 | 0.0 |
| *Campylo-bacter* spp. | 1,963,141 | 14.2 | 10,539 | 17.3 | 99 | 5.5 |
| *E. coli O157: H7* | 62,458 | 0.5 | 1,843 | 3.0 | 52 | 2.9 |

*(continues)*

## ESTIMATED FREQUENCIES OF ILLNESSES, HOSPITALIZATIONS, AND DEATHS OF CERTAIN FOOD-BORNE PATHOGENS IN THE UNITED STATES *(continued)* ▶

| AGENT | ILLNESSES | | HOSPITALIZATIONS | | DEATHS | |
|---|---|---|---|---|---|---|
| | TOTAL | PERCENT* | TOTAL | PERCENT* | TOTAL | PERCENT* |
| *Listeria monocyto-genes* | 2,493 | 0.0 | 2,298 | 3.8 | 499 | 27.6 |
| *Salmonella* non-typhoidal | 1,341,873 | 9.7 | 15,608 | 25.6 | 553 | 30.6 |
| *Streptococcus* food-borne | 50,920 | 0.4 | 358 | 0.6 | 0 | 0.0 |
| *Yersina enterocolitica* | 86,731 | 0.6 | 1,105 | 1.8 | 2 | 0.1 |

*(continues)*

# ▲ ESTIMATED FREQUENCIES OF ILLNESSES, HOSPITALIZATIONS, AND DEATHS OF CERTAIN FOOD-BORNE PATHOGENS IN THE UNITED STATES  *(continued)*  ▷

| AGENT | ILLNESSES | | HOSPITALIZATIONS | | DEATHS | |
|---|---|---|---|---|---|---|
| | TOTAL | PERCENT* | TOTAL | PERCENT* | TOTAL | PERCENT* |
| Parasitic | | | | | | |
| *Crytosporidium parvum* | 30,000 | 0.2 | 199 | 0.3 | 7 | 0.4 |
| *Giardia lamblia* | 200,000 | 1.4 | 500 | 0.8 | 1 | 0.1 |
| *Toxoplasma gondii* | 112,500 | 0.8 | 2,500 | 4.1 | 375 | 20.7 |

*(continues)*

## ◁ ESTIMATED FREQUENCIES OF ILLNESSES, HOSPITALIZATIONS, AND DEATHS OF CERTAIN FOOD-BORNE PATHOGENS IN THE UNITED STATES *(continued)* ▷

| AGENT | ILLNESSES | | HOSPITALIZATIONS | | DEATHS | |
|---|---|---|---|---|---|---|
| | TOTAL | PERCENT* | TOTAL | PERCENT* | TOTAL | PERCENT* |
| Viral | | | | | | |
| Norwalk-like viruses | 9,200,000 | 66.6 | 20,000 | 32.9 | 124 | 6.9 |
| Rotavirus | 39,000 | 0.3 | 500 | 0.8 | 0 | 0.0 |
| Astrovirus | 39,000 | 0.3 | 125 | 0.2 | 0 | 0.0 |
| Hepatitis A | 4,170 | 0.0 | 90 | 0.9 | 4 | 0.2 |

*Percent of all food-borne illnesses

Source: Paul S. Mead, et al., "Food-Related Illness and Death in the United States," *Emerging Infectious Diseases*, September–October 1999, 607–617, p. 611.

## ◁ SOME FOOD-BORNE BACTERIAL DISEASE OUTBREAKS IN 2004 ▷

| AGENT | STATE | NUMBER ILL | VEHICLE | LOCATION |
|---|---|---|---|---|
| *Bacillus cereus* | Conn. | 11 | Chicken, roasted | Senior center |
| *Campylobacter jejuni* | Iowa | 32 | Whole milk, unpasteur-ized | Lodge dinner event |
| *Clostridium perfringens* | Mich. | 56 | Spaghetti, unspecified | Private home |
| *Escherichia coli O157: NM* | Ga. | 2 | Alfalfa sprout | Restaurant or delicatessen |
| *Salmonella anatum* | N.Y. | 108 | Roast beef, other | Picnic |
| *Salmonella enteritidis* | Pa. | 4 | Eggs, over easy | Restaurant or delicatessen |
| *Salmonella heidelberg* | Calif. | 78 | Sandwich, turkey | Restaurant, delicatessen, private home, workplace |
| *Salmonella newport* | Wisc. | 13 | Unspecified | Nursing home |
| *Salmonella typhimurium* | Calif. | 23 | Turkey, un-specified | Prison |
| *Shigella flexneri* | N.J. | 6 | Macaroni salad, cole-slaw, potato salad | Restaurant or delicatessen |
| *Staphylococcus aureus* | Ohio | 132 | Ice cream, commercial | Restaurant or delicatessen; private home |

Source: Food-Borne Outbreaks due to Bacterial Etiologies, 2004. Available online. URL: http://www.cdc.gov/foodborneoutbreaks/us_outb/fbo2004/Outbreak_Linelist_Final_2004.pdf.

number of people involved, the dates of the incident, characteristics of those who have become ill, and laboratory results obtained during the outbreak. The table on page 139 lists a few examples of the more than 1,200 outbreaks of food-borne illness reported in the United States in 2004, the last year for which data are available.

Researchers have observed a significant change in the pathogens most commonly involved in food-borne illnesses in the United States. At the beginning of the 20th century, the most common food-borne illnesses in the United States were typhoid fever, tuberculosis, and cholera. But improvements in food safety practices (such as the use of chlorine to purify public water supplies, better methods of food canning and preservation, and pasteurization of milk) led to dramatic decreases in the number of cases of food-borne illnesses caused by these pathogens. The graph below shows, for example, changes in the incidence of typhoid fever in the United States between 1920 and 1960. The changes shown in this graph are typical of those for other traditional food-borne illnesses, like tuberculosis and cholera. (The graph ends at 1960 because the number of deaths from typhoid fever reached nearly zero in that year and has remained very low ever since.)

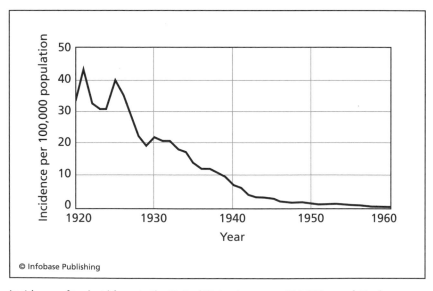

© Infobase Publishing

Incidence of typhoid fever in the United States (cases per 100,000 population)

Changes in the etiology of food-borne illnesses have been fairly dramatic even in recent decades. Prior to the 1980s, pathogens of considerable importance today, such as *E. coli 0157:H7, Listeria monocytogenes,* and *Camplyobacter jejuni,* were not even recognized as possible causes of food-borne illnesses. Today, all three pathogens are known to be responsible for significant numbers of food-borne illness outbreaks.

Even since the mid-1990s, a number of new pathogens have been detected in contaminated foods. In 1996, for example, a parasite called *Cyclospora cayetanensis,* first observed in a shipment of raspberries from Guatemala, was found to be responsible for an outbreak of diarrheal illness among people who had eaten the berries. Two years later, a new strain of the bacterium *Vibrio parahemolyticus* was detected in oysters taken from a bed in Galveston Bay. As the 1999 Mead survey of food-borne illnesses suggests, pathogens have still not been identified for a large majority of outbreaks in the United States.

## Prevention of Food-Borne Illnesses

Knowledge of how agents that cause food-borne illnesses get into food makes it possible to outline procedures to prevent such illnesses. Pathogens, for example, survive and grow in foods only under certain favorable environmental conditions, such as a warm temperature, the presence of moisture, and neutral acidity (pH of about 7.0). People can decrease the likelihood that pathogens will remain in foods, then, by treating those foods so as to eliminate favorable conditions, for example, by keeping foods cold or hot. In the case of physical impurities that sometimes make their way into foods— such as bone, glass, wood, metal, and plastic—the most important preventive steps involve greater attention to methods of processing and packaging foods. For example, the presence of bone fragments in food generally means that mechanisms used to process meat do not adequately separate meat from bone and/or do not sufficiently pulverize bone that is to remain in the meat product.

By far the most important food safety procedures, however, are those that prevent the growth of pathogens in food or destroy those pathogens already present. All states and the vast majority of communities now have strict guidelines for the training and testing of individuals who are involved in food preparation and presentation in public facilities (although no such regulations deal with food handling in private homes). Those guidelines usually contain, at a minimum, the following basic elements of safe handling of foods: rigorous personal hygiene, thorough cooking, proper refrigeration, and keeping raw and cooked foods separate.

One of the most critical sources of food-borne illnesses is poor personal hygiene. Food handlers have a number of opportunities to transmit pathogens from some external source to the foods with which they work. These risks can be greatly reduced by one simple practice: hand-washing. Most food-handling guidelines suggest that a person wash his or her hands well after using the bathroom; after sneezing, coughing, or blowing one's nose; after eating, drinking, or smoking; after taking out garbage or handling it in any other way; after using any chemical intended for cleaning purposes; and before and after handling raw foods.

A second simple approach to avoiding food-borne illnesses is to make sure that foods are cooked adequately before being served and then stored at a safe temperature. All pathogens are killed if they are heated to a high enough temperature for a long enough time, although the specific temperature and time needed varies for various pathogens. For example, poultry must be cooked to a temperature of at least 165°F (74°C), while pork, beef, and fish need be cooked to only 145°F (63°C).

The *food danger zone* is the range of temperatures within which pathogens survive and reproduce most efficiently, between about 40°F (4°C) and 140°F (60°C). At temperatures below 40°F (4°C), pathogens *may* be killed or they may simply be inactivated. At temperatures above 140°F (60°C), most common pathogens are killed. This fact provides a reasonable rule of thumb for knowing when pathogens are likely to be absent from food (when it is heated to temperatures greater than 140°F [60°C]), and when they are likely to remain inactive (when food is cooled to temperatures below 40°F [4°C]). It also provides the basis for a number of common guidelines for the handling and storage of foods:

> ➤ Cool foods as quickly as possible before they are stored, for example, by placing them in an ice bath or the refrigerator. Rapid cooling reduces the time that those foods will remain in the food danger zone.

> ➤ Stir foods as they are being cooled. Stirring allows an increase of cool air around the foods and allows them to pass through the food danger zone more quickly.

> ➤ If possible, cut food into small pieces to accelerate the rate of cooling.

> ➤ Foods that must be reheated should be heated as quickly as possible, again allowing them to remain in the food danger zone for the shortest period of time.

The term *cross-contamination* means the transfer of pathogens from one food to another, either directly or indirectly. For example, a food worker may begin to make a salad on a table where he or she has just cut up a raw chicken. If the worker does not take precautions, pathogens present in the chicken may be transferred to the salad. The chicken itself will probably be cooked to a temperature sufficient to kill pathogens, but the salad will not, and consumers may be exposed to those pathogens indirectly. To avoid cross-contamination, food handlers are required to clean thoroughly (sanitize) all areas that have been exposed to potential pathogen-bearing food products.

Ensuring that food handlers know about and practice safety procedures such as the ones described above is the best way of ensuring that food is free of the pathogens responsible for food-borne illnesses. These procedures are equally valid whether practiced in large commercial kitchens or in private homes.

# Regulating Food Safety

Protecting citizens from food-borne illnesses like those described above is a priority for governmental agencies at all levels, from federal to local governments. Because food safety is important to all levels of government, laws and regulations are often complex and overlapping. At the federal level, the regulation of food safety is a large operation shared by four major agencies: The Food and Drug Administration (FDA), part of the Department of Health and Human Services (DHHS); the Food Safety and Inspection Service (FSIS) and the Animal and Plant Health Inspection Service (APHIS), both part of the U.S. Department of Agriculture (USDA); and the Environmental Protection Agency (EPA). Other agencies that have roles in ensuring the safety of foods include the National Marine Fisheries Service (NMFS), part of the Department of Commerce; the Grain Inspection, Packers and Stockyard Administration (GIPSA) of the USDA; and the Centers for Disease Control and Prevention (CDC) of the DHHS.

The EPA's role in food safety is primarily limited to monitoring pesticide use in plants and animals grown for food and protecting the quality of the nation's water quality, a large part of which is used to raise food crops and animals. The EPA's responsibilities in monitoring food safety arise primarily from authority provided in the Federal Insecticide, Fungicide, and Rodenticide Act (FIFRA), passed in 1947, which regulates the use of pesticides.

Regulation of beef, pork, poultry, and a few other meat products is the responsibility of the USDA, while the FDA monitors most other food products, including fruits and vegetables, seafood, eggs, and milk. The FDA's statutory responsibilities for food safety date to the passage of the Pure Food and Drug Act of 1906 (PFDA), by which the agency was created. Those responsibilities have been enlarged and refined in a number of amendments to the original PFDA. Among the FDA's many food safety responsibilities are monitoring the safety of food additives, providing consumer education and industry outreach on issues of food safety, overseeing the safety of foods developed through biotechnology (such as genetically modified foods), ensuring that foods are properly labeled, and carrying out research programs on food-borne illnesses. An important agency within the FDA that deals with food safety issues is the Center for Food Safety and Applied Nutrition. The FDA also includes a comparable agency responsible for monitoring food products fed to animals, the Center for Veterinary Medicine.

Various agencies of the USDA are responsible for conducting on-site inspections of food-production facilities as the result of a number of federal laws designed to protect the safety of specific food products. Among these laws are the Federal Meat Inspection Act of 1906 (FMIA), the Poultry Products Inspection Act of 1957 (PPIA), the Egg Products Inspection Act of 1970 (EPIA), the Food Quality Protection Act of 1996 (FQPA), and the Public Health Service Act of 1944 (PHSA) and its amendments. The two USDA agencies responsible for enforcing these laws are the Food Safety and Inspection Service (FSIS) and the Animal and Plant Health Inspection Service (APHIS). The FSIS establishes requirements for certain slaughter and food-processing activities (such as plant sanitation and thermal processing) and for labeling of meat and poultry products. It carries out chemical, microbiological, and other tests at food-processing plants, and it works with the CDC to investigate outbreaks of food-borne illnesses. The FSIS also maintains a program of inspection for foods imported to the United States from other nations and periodically reviews the safety requirements of exporting nations. It conducts similar reviews of state requirements to make sure that they are at least equivalent to federal standards.

The Animal and Plant Health Inspection Service (APHIS) is responsible for protecting agriculture in the United States from the entry, establishment, and/or spread of animal and plant pests and noxious weeds. It carries out its work through six primary agencies: Animal Care, Plant Protection and Quarantine, Veterinary Services, Wildlife Services, International Services, and Biotechnology Regulatory Services. The last two of these divisions have grown increasingly important in recent years. Biotechnology Regulatory Services is responsible for testing and monitoring genetically modified foods in the United States, and International Services carries out testing of foods to be imported to the United States. In 2003, the APHIS had offices in 27 foreign countries on six continents, employing more than 300 experts in food safety and inspection. Their duties are to carry out programs of surveillance, eradication, and control in countries that harbor economically significant pests or diseases, such as the Mediterranean fruit fly (Mexico, Guatemala),

Mexican fruit fly (Mexico), boll weevil (Mexico), carambola fruit fly and tropical bont tick (Caribbean islands), hydrilla (Mexico), screw-worm (Panama), and foot-and-mouth disease (Mexico, Colombia, Central America, and Panama).

An aspect of food safety regulation in the United States with which consumer groups sometimes take issue is that federal and state agencies seldom have the authority to order recalls of contaminated food products. They may issue warnings to food-processing facilities, request intervention from the courts, and encourage food processors, distributors, and sellers to withdraw contaminated products from the market, but they are not able to take those actions themselves. In practice, however, food companies seldom ignore requests and recommendations of regulatory agencies with regard to contaminated food.

When food products are found to be unsafe for human consumption, the company that grew or processed them has several possible courses of action under FDA guidelines:

➤ *Stock recovery,* in which stores return food products to processors even though there may be nothing wrong with the products. They may, for example, simply have gone past the recommended "sell-by" date, and stores may no longer be willing to stock the items.

➤ *Market withdrawals,* in which a product never leaves the food-processing facility but is no longer made available to retailers (for any number of reasons).

➤ *Corrections,* in which retailers make changes to food labels without the products being returned to the food-processing facility. Corrections do not involve label changes in foods that are unfit for human consumption.

➤ *Recalls,* which are requested by a food-processing company when it learns that something about the food makes it unsuitable for human consumption. Three levels of recalls are recommended by the FDA:

Class I, in which there is a strong likelihood that ingestion of a food may result in serious health problems or death. Contaminations with *Listeria monocytogenes, Clostridium botulinum,* or *E. coli 0157: H7,* for example, would prompt a Class I recall.

Class II, in which contamination of a food product may result in relatively mild health consequences but is not likely to produce either serious health consequences or death. Contaminations caused by most species of the *Salmonella* bacterium and by unapproved food additives are likely to prompt a Class II recall.

Class III, in which the contaminated food is expected to result in the least harmful health problems, if any. For example, foods are sometimes simply mislabeled and have to be recalled for corrections in the label.

As this section indicates, an extensive network of safety programs has developed over the past century to guarantee the safety of foods grown, sold, and consumed in the United States. All states and many local governments also have laws and regulations that augment the federal program, ensuring that foods consumed in the United States are among the safest in the world.

## Surveys of Domestic Food Safety

Regulatory agencies are required by law or administrative rules to report the number of food inspections they have conducted and the results of those inspections. The FSIS, for example, issues an annual report on its activities to Congress, while the FDA issues irregular reports on its inspections of fruits and vegetables, milk and egg products, and seafood. In its 2000 report, the most recent available, the FSIS reported that it had inspected more than 130 million meat animals and 8.5 billion poultry animals in 2000. As shown in the table on page 148, the percentage of animals condemned as unsafe for human consumption ranged from less than 0.2 percent for sheep to more than 3 percent for turkeys.

| ◀ FSIS INSPECTION ACTIVITIES, 2000 ▶ | | | |
|---|---|---|---|
| SPECIES | NUMBER OF ANIMALS INSPECTED | NUMBER CONDEMNED | PERCENTAGE CONDEMNED |
| cattle | 35,136,375 | 188,914 | 0.54 |
| calves | 1,103,173 | 22,408 | 2.03 |
| swine | 93,385,041 | 410,814 | 0.44 |
| goats | 530,371 | 1,247 | 0.24 |
| sheep | 3,315,532 | 5,831 | 0.18 |
| equines | 50,449 | 254 | 0.50 |
| other livestock | 19,065 | 20 | 0.10 |
| total livestock | 133,540,006 | 629,488 | 0.47 |
| young chickens | 8,082,064,151 | 82,350,929 | 1.02 |
| mature chickens | 169,679,149 | 10,073,129 | 5.94 |
| fryer-roaster turkeys | 166,026 | 2,687 | 1.62 |
| young turkeys | 259,739,860 | 1,737,600 | 0.67 |

*(continues)*

| ◄ FSIS INSPECTION ACTIVITIES, 2000 *(continued)* ► | | | |
|---|---|---|---|
| SPECIES | NUMBER OF ANIMALS INSPECTED | NUMBER CONDEMNED | PERCENTAGE CONDEMNED |
| mature turkeys | 2,133,739 | 73,851 | 3.46 |
| ducks | 23,784,714 | 453,296 | 1.91 |
| other poultry | 9,704,016 | 66,163 | 0.68 |
| total poultry | 8,547,271,655 | 94,757,665 | 1.11 |

Source: "Meat, Poultry, and Egg Products Inspection: 2000 Report of the Secretary of Agriculture to the U.S. Congress." Available online. URL: http://www.fsis.usda. gov/oa/pubs/rtc2000/report.pdf.

Inspection of the nation's fruit and vegetable food products has been more sporadic. Probably the broadest survey of such products taken in recent years was one conducted by the FDA in March 2000. Some results of that survey are shown in the table on pages 150–151. That survey was initiated to satisfy a 1997 directive issued by President Bill Clinton "to provide further assurance that fruits and vegetables consumed by the American public meet the highest health and safety standards." President's Clinton directive, in turn, was motivated by a joint report prepared by a committee of the DHHS, USDA, and EPA indicating that the safety of fresh produce in the United States was an area of growing concern. The 2000 FDA survey showed that while the rate of contaminated fruits and vegetables from domestic sources was very low, imported products

# ◁ SURVEY OF FRUIT AND VEGETABLE CONTAMINATION, 2000 ▷

| PRODUCE ITEM | IMPORTED PRODUCE SURVEY* | | | DOMESTIC PRODUCE SURVEY** | | |
|---|---|---|---|---|---|---|
| | NUMBER SAMPLED | NUMBER POSITIVE *** | PERCENT VIOLATION | NUMBER SAMPLED | NUMBER POSITIVE*** | PERCENT VIOLATION |
| cantaloupe | 151 | 11 | 7.3 | 164 | 5 | 3.0 |
| celery | 84 | 3 | 3.6 | 120 | 0 | 0.0 |
| cilantro | 177 | 16 | 9.0 | 85 | 1 | 1.2 |
| culantro**** | 12 | 6 | 50.0 | 0 | 0 | 0.0 |
| lettuce | 116 | 2 | 1.7 | 142 | 1 | 0.7 |
| parsley | 84 | 2 | 2.4 | 90 | 1 | 0.0 |

*(continues)*

# ◁ SURVEY OF FRUIT AND VEGETABLE CONTAMINATION, 2000 (continued) ▷

| PRODUCE ITEM | IMPORTED PRODUCE SURVEY* | | | DOMESTIC PRODUCE SURVEY** | | |
|---|---|---|---|---|---|---|
| | NUMBER SAMPLED | NUMBER POSITIVE*** | PERCENT VIOLATION | NUMBER SAMPLED | NUMBER POSITIVE*** | PERCENT VIOLATION |
| scallions | 180 | 3 | 1.7 | 93 | 3 | 3.2 |
| strawberries | 143 | 1 | 0.7 | 136 | 0 | 0.0 |
| tomatoes | 20 | 0 | 0.0 | 198 | 0 | 0.0 |

*Survey conducted in fiscal year (FY) 1999 on 1,003 samples.

**Survey conducted in FY 2000/2001 on 1,028 samples.

***Positive = contaminated with a pathogen.

****Culantro is a cilantro-like herb from the Caribbean.

Source: Adapted from "FDA Survey of Domestic Fresh Produce, FY2000/2001 Field Assignment." Available online. URL: http://vm.cfsan.fda.gov/~dms/prodsu10.html.

were a very different matter, with as much as half of such products contaminated.

Regular food inspections are an essential part of food safety programs. They provide government officials with information on the percentage of food products that are contaminated and places where contamination may be a problem. This information allows more vigorous enforcement of existing laws and regulations and, where needed, the adoption of new laws and regulations.

# Issues of Imported Food Safety

One of the most serious problems facing government officials involved with protecting the safety of Americans' foods is the dramatic increase in the amount of food products imported from countries around the world. As numerous studies have shown, federal and state agencies have done a remarkable job of ensuring the safety of domestically grown food, no mater the type of food, its origin, or its manner of preparation. But as of the early 21st century, the rapidly increasing globalization of the food industry has added yet another level of complexity to the process of ensuring food safety. Today, virtually any food grown or raised anywhere in the world can be made available for sale anywhere else in the world. Instead of getting strawberries from the farm next door or a farm in Arizona, for instance, Americans now purchase strawberries grown almost exclusively in some foreign country, usually Mexico. Ensuring the safety of imported food products at a level equivalent to that established for domestic products has become a real challenge for American health officials.

The FDA estimated in a 2003 report that the United States now imports food from at least 100 different countries. Imports make up at least 10 percent of all the food Americans eat, and for some commodities such as fresh fruits and vegetables that number is more than 40 percent. These numbers have risen rapidly in the past few decades as food distribution has become a globalized business, much as other types of businesses have. The FDA report said that the number of food entries to the United States from other nations had doubled between 1996 and 2003, and it projected that the rate of increase would continue to grow even more rapidly. It estimated an increase of 30 percent in the importation of foods in fiscal year 2002.

One of the fundamental problems in monitoring the safety of imported food products is that other nations do not always have the financial, technical, political, and other frameworks necessary to maintain a food safety system comparable to that of the United States. So food shipped to the United States is *inherently* more likely to be contaminated than that coming from domestic sources. Adding to this problem are international trade agreements that require one country to accept the imports of another country as essentially equivalent in safety to their domestic counterparts.

Such trade agreements are proliferating. The North American Free Trade Agreement (NAFTA), for example, contains an equivalency provision. The treaty's three signatories, Canada, the United States, and Mexico, have all agreed to accept the food inspection systems in place in the three nations as equivalent to one another. NAFTA essentially ignores issues of food safety. It establishes no minimum food safety standards and does not require member nations to have any such standards. It relies instead on each nation's voluntary efforts to ensure the safety of the foods it produces.

Agreements developed within the context of the World Trade Organization (WTO) have similar problems. According to some studies, the United States has imported foods from other nations that do not meet U.S. domestic safety standards as a result of the principle of equivalency of food inspection systems among all signatories to WTO trade agreements. The Global Trade Watch project of Public Citizen (a nonprofit consumer advocacy group), for example, found that some of the 4 billion pounds of meat and poultry products imported under WTO trade agreements from Argentina, Australia, Brazil, Canada, and Mexico in 2002 did not meet U.S. food safety standards.

The lack of satisfactory inspections of imported foods is a matter of some dispute. Data do suggest, however, that such foods have been responsible for a number of outbreaks of food-borne disease in the United States and elsewhere over the past two decades. For example, in 1997, nearly two dozen outbreaks of the food-borne disease cyclosporiasis were reported in eight states (California, Florida,

Maryland, Nebraska, Nevada, New York, Rhode Island, and Texas) and one Canadian province (Ontario). Over a two-month period, more than 500 confirmed and suspected cases of the disease were traced to the ingestion of raspberries apparently imported from Guatemala. The previous year, a similar series of outbreaks had taken place in which more than 1,000 cases of the disease had been reported. Although the precise source of contamination was never determined, investigators suspected that the raspberries had been sprayed with an insecticide or fungicide made with impure water.

Even individuals who try to eat a completely healthy diet cannot be sure that the foods they ingest will be totally safe. In 1995, for example, an outbreak of illnesses caused by the bacterium *Salmonella stanley* in 17 U.S. states and Finland was traced to alfalfa sprouts imported from the Netherlands. While just 242 cases were identified in the two nations, extrapolating from usual reporting patterns, experts estimated that between 5,000 and 24,000 individuals had actually been infected by the bacterium. The 1995 incident was only the most recent in which bacterial contamination of sprouts led to outbreaks of food-borne illnesses in Canada, Denmark, Finland, Sweden, the United Kingdom, and the United States. The table on pages 155–156 summarizes some other outbreaks of food-borne illnesses in the United States that have been traced to foods imported from other nations.

U.S. agencies responsible for food safety attempt to deal with the imports problem in a variety of ways. For example, they often establish agreements with countries that export food to the United States allowing U.S. officials to inspect the food safety systems of those countries. The FDA conducted the first of these food safety audits in 1998, when inspectors monitored systems in Honduras and Trinidad and Tobago. In 1999, food safety programs in four more nations—Costa Rica, El Salvador, Guatemala, and Nicaragua—were audited. The FDA suspended inspections of foreign food safety systems in 2000, however, when the agency had to redirect its resources to other international programs.

Federal agencies also monitor imported foods by inspecting food arrivals at American ports. The problem is that the volume of imported food is so large that only a small fraction is ever inspected,

## ◁ SELECTED EXAMPLES OF FOOD-BORNE ILLNESS OUTBREAKS IN THE UNITED STATES ▷

| YEAR | PATHOGEN | FOOD VEHICLE | NUMBER OF CASES (CONFIRMED) | ORIGIN OF COMMODITY |
|------|----------|--------------|----------------------------|---------------------|
| 1988 | hepatitis A virus | Lettuce | 202 | Mexico |
| 1989 | Salmonella | Cantaloupe | 25,000 | Mexico |
| 1990 | E. coli O157:H7 | Scallops | 1,400 | South America |
| 1991 | Salmonella | Cantaloupe | 400 | Mexico |
| 1992 | Histamine poisoning | Tuna | 74 | Ecuador |
| 1994 | Shigella | Green onions | 171 | Mexico |
| 1995 | Salmonella | Alfalfa sprouts | 242 | Netherlands |
| 1996 | Cyclospora | Raspberries | 1,465 | Guatemala |

*(continues)*

## ◁ SELECTED EXAMPLES OF FOOD-BORNE ILLNESS OUTBREAKS IN THE UNITED STATES *(continued)* ▷

| YEAR | PATHOGEN | FOOD VEHICLE | NUMBER OF CASES (CONFIRMED) | ORIGIN OF COMMODITY |
|------|----------|--------------|----------------------------|---------------------|
| 1996 | *E. coli 0157:H7* | Lettuce | 27 | Australia |
| 1997 | hepatitis A virus | Strawberries | 270 | Mexico |
| 1997 | *Cyclospora* | Raspberries | 1,012 | Guatemala |
| 1997 | *Salmonella saphra* | Cantaloupe | 24 | Mexico |
| 1998 | *Shigella sonnei* | Parsley | 342 | Mexico |
| 1999 | *Salmonella* | Mango | 72 | Brazil |

Source: Adapted from data in Food Safety Network for May 11, 1998 (http://131.104.232.9/fsnet/1998/5-1998/fs-05-11-98-01.txt) and other sources.

no more than about 2 percent of all food imports. The USDA, FDA, and other agencies try to make these inspections more efficient by focusing on foods and nations that appear to be especially likely sources of contaminated imports. As the volume of imported foods increases, so does the need for inspectors. In 2002, for example, the FDA hired 300 new inspectors to monitor food imports, doubling the number of examinations conducted from 12,000 in 2001 to 24,000 in 2002. It doubled that number again in 2003, conducting 48,000 inspections, but made no further increases in 2004.

The problem of foreign food safety increased exponentially after the September 11, 2001, terrorist attacks. American officials became suddenly and keenly aware of the many different ways that terrorists could attack Americans. One of the most obvious would be to intentionally contaminate foods shipped to the United States with a pathogen that could produce a widespread epidemic. In response to this possibility, the U.S. Congress passed the Public Health Security and Bioterrorism Preparedness and Response Act of 2002 (the Bioterrorism Act), which President Bush signed into law on June 12, 2002. Title III of that act deals with protection of the nation's food system, especially the monitoring of foods imported from other nations. Agencies already responsible for monitoring food safety, such as the USDA and FDA, were instructed to expand their activities to improve their regulation of foods being brought into the country.

For example, the FDA was charged with overseeing the safety of food shipments into the United States. In response, the agency developed a program known as Prior Notice of Imported Food Shipments (PNIFS). Under this program, companies that intend to ship foods into the United States must first notify the FDA of their intent and provide detailed information about the nature of the food shipment. The FDA uses this information before the food's arrival to determine whether to inspect the imported food. The new PNIFS system went into effect on December 12, 2003.

Problems of guaranteeing the safety of imported foods are likely to grow in the future. As globalization of the food industry continues to grow, a large fraction of the food Americans eat will continue to come from virtually every nation in the world. Maintaining safety comparable to U.S. standards for these foods will be a challenge. Ongoing threats of bioterrorism will also remain a concern for the foreseeable future. Based on the nation's experience of the past decade, existing programs appear to be adequate to meet those challenges, provided that the federal government continues to provide the funds necessary to allow them to operate at maximum efficiency.

## One Solution: Irradiated Food?

For nearly a century, some scientists have been suggesting that an effective way of killing the pathogens that cause food-borne illnesses is with radiation. The history of irradiated food dates to 1895, when the German physicist Wilhelm Conrad Roentgen (1845–1923) discovered the existence of X-rays, a high-energy form of electromagnetic radiation with great penetrating power. Less than a year later, a colleague of Roentgen by the name of Minsch suggested that X-rays could be used to kill the pathogens that cause food-borne illnesses. Less than a decade later, the first experiments on radiation's ability to destroy microorganisms were carried out by Samuel Cate Prescott (1872–1962), a bacteriologist at the Massachusetts Institute of Technology. At the time, canned foods were notoriously unsafe, with up to half of some products containing some level of pathogens. Prescott found that gamma rays emitted by radium metal killed bacteria and argued that irradiating foods might provide a safer alternative to the more widely used practice of canning. Prescott had barely published his research on the irradiation of foods before the first two patents were issued to other people for commercial applications of the process, one in Great Britain and one in the United States.

The sources of radiation needed were far too expensive to use on a commercial scale, however. As a result, relatively little research on *food irradiation* was done over the next four decades. One exception of particular interest was a series of experiments carried out by Benjamin Schwartz, Chief of the Zoological Division of the USDA's Bureau of Animal Industry. Schwartz's long-standing special interest was trichinosis, a disease of international concern caused by infestation of pork by the *Trichinella spiralis* worm. Schwartz found that X-rays were very efficient in killing *Trichinella,* providing an excellent way to protect consumers from a serious food-borne illness. Although Schwartz received a patent for his discovery, the method he developed was not widely used. It was much more expensive than the simpler procedure of simply cooking pork to a high enough temperature to kill the pathogen.

The potential of food irradiation as a method to prevent the spread of food-borne illnesses received renewed attention in the late 1940s as the new field of nuclear energy rapidly expanded. By the end of World War II, scientists had begun to develop relatively inexpensive sources of radiation that could be used on a large enough scale to make food irradiation commercially viable. One of the first organizations to take an interest in the process was the U.S. Army, which saw it as a possible method for preserving foods for troops in the field. In 1953, the Army created the National Food Irradiation Program (NFIP), a series of tests designed to assess the effectiveness of low levels of radiation in the preservation of various types of food. The Atomic Energy Commission (AEC) soon joined the Army as a sponsor of the NFIP. From 1955 to 1965, the Army Medical Department carried out an extensive program of research on the irradiation of 21 foods. The National Food Irradiation Program remained in operation until 1980.

The first nation to approve food irradiation for commercial use was West Germany, which, in 1957, authorized the irradiation of spices used in the manufacture of sausages. The government changed course only a year later, however, and declared a ban on the use of radiation on any food products. The first nation to sustain approval of food irradiation was the former Soviet Union. In 1958, the Soviet government announced that the irradiation of potatoes to prevent sprouting was permissible; a year later it extended approval to the irradiation of grain for the purpose of disinfestation. In 1960, Canada first approved irradiated foods when it authorized the use of radiation to prevent sprouting in potatoes.

In 1958, Congress gave the Food and Drug Administration regulatory responsibility for food irradiation in the United States. Congress declared that irradiation was to be regarded as a food additive subject to all regulations already in place for that category. Over the

## ◄ SAMUEL CATE PRESCOTT (1872–1962) ►

The chemical and bacteriological principles of food preservation; diseases of the banana plant; chemistry of the roasting and preparation of coffee; studies of the irradiation of foods for the purpose of preservation; bacteriology of water supplies; preparation of dehydrated and quick-frozen foods; the history of the Massachusetts Institute of Technology—these are among the topics to which Samuel Cate Prescott turned his attention during his lifetime. It is not difficult to see why his contemporaries saw him as a man of enormous energy who never seemed to run out of research topics about which he wanted to learn more, a why members of the food technology community often refer to him as one of the "fathers" of modern food technology.

Samuel Cate Prescott was born on a farm in rural New Hampshire near the town of South Hampton on April 5, 1872. After completing his secondary education in New Hampshire, he enrolled at the Massachusetts Institute of Technology (MIT), where he specialized in microbiology, industrial biology, food sciences and technology, and public health. He earned his bachelor's degree from MIT in 1894.

Upon graduation, Prescott took a position in teaching and research at MIT, which he held for the rest of his academic career. A major focus of his research was on chemistry and bacteriology of food canning, which, according to biographer Cecil G. Dunn, "did much to put the canning of food on a sound scientific basis." In addition to his research activities, Prescott

next decade, the FDA approved a small number of applications for the irradiation of foods, including

➤   sterilization of bacon (for the U.S. Army) in 1963,

➤   disinfestation of wheat and flour in 1963,

➤   prevention of sprouting in white potatoes in 1964, and

➤   sterilization of various packaging materials in 1971.

devoted much of his time and energy to lecturing and writing for both the professional community and the lay public about methods of food preservation.

During his long career at MIT, Prescott held a number of administrative positions. In 1922 he was appointed head of the Department of Biology and Public Health. A decade later, he was chosen as the first dean of MIT's School of Science, a post he held until his retirement in 1942. Prescott was also active in a number of other academic and professional organizations. From 1904 to 1921, he served as director of the Boston Biochemical Laboratory, and prior to World War I he served as a staff member at the Sanitary Research Laboratory and Sewage Experimentation Station in Boston. During the war, Prescott was commissioned as a major in the Sanitary Corps of the U.S. Army, where he studied problems of maintaining food quality for troops serving at the battle front. During World War II, Prescott served as a consultant to the Office of the Quartermaster General on problems of food dehydration.

In addition to his many speaking engagements, Prescott wrote widely for both the professional and general audience. His works included a translation of Jean Effront's classic *Enzymes and Their Applications* (1902), a revision of William T. Sedgwick's popular *Principles of Sanitary Science and Public Health* (1935; with Murray P. Horwood), *Industrial Microbiology* (1940; with Cecil G. Dunn), *Water Bacteriology* (1946), and *When M.I.T. Was Boston Tech* (1954). Prescott was a charter member of the Society of American Bacteriologists and one of the founders and the first president (1941) of the Institute of Food Technologists. He died in Boston on March 19, 1962.

As of 2004, federal approval had been granted for the irradiation of 16 types of foods, from herbs and spices to animal feed and pet food. The table on pages 162–163 lists items for which radiation has been approved.

Food irradiation was also being used to protect food supplies in a number of other nations. The table on pages 164–165 provides some examples of this practice.

The potential for using radiation as a way of destroying pathogens in food has been known for more than a century. Still, progress has been slow in using this technology to protect food safety. For many years, the cost of irradiation equipment delayed adoption of

### ◄ APPROVED USES OF IRRADIATION IN FOODS IN THE UNITED STATES ►

| PRODUCT | PURPOSE | YEAR APPROVED |
|---|---|---|
| **Low dose (less than 1 kGy*)** | | |
| wheat and wheat flour | insect control | 1963 |
| white potatoes | sprouting inhibition | 1964 |
| pork | control of *Trichinella spiralis* | 1985 |
| fruit | insect control; delay of ripening | 1986 |
| fresh vegetables' | insect control | 1986 |
| **Medium dose (1–10 kGy)** | | |
| dehydrated enzymes | control of microbes | 1986 |
| meat, uncooked and chilled | control of microbes | 1997 |
| meat, uncooked and frozen | control of microbes | 1997 |
| poultry, fresh and frozen | control of microbes | 1990 |
| seeds for sprouting | control of microbes | 2000 |
| shell eggs | control of *Salmonella* | 2000 |

*(continues)*

◁  **APPROVED USES OF IRRADIATION IN FOODS IN
THE UNITED STATES** *(continued)*  ▷

| PRODUCT | PURPOSE | YEAR APPROVED |
|---|---|---|
| High dose (11–45 kGy) | | |
| herbs | control of microbes | 1986 |
| spices | control of microbes | 1986 |
| vegetable-seasonings | control of microbes | 1986 |
| meat, frozen and packaged | sterilization | 1995 |
| animal feed and pet food | control of *Salmonella* | 1995 |

*kGy = kilograys, a unit for the measurement of radiation energy.
Source: Adapted from J. Lynne Brown, "How Safe Are Irradiated Foods?" College of Agricultural Sciences, Pennsylvania State University, 2002. Available online. URL: http://pubs.cas.psu.edu/freepubs/pdfs/uk109.pdf.

the practice. In recent years, other factors, such as the availability of other technologies and public resistance to the use of radiation, have continued to inhibit the spread of food irradiation practices.

## Methods of Food Irradiation

All methods of food irradiation operate on a common chemical principle: Destruction of certain critical molecules in an organism, such as enzyme

## ◄ WORLDWIDE APPROVED USES OF IRRADIATED FOODS ►

| COUNTRY | FOOD PRODUCT(S) |
| --- | --- |
| Argentina | spices, spinach, cocoa powder |
| Bangladesh | potatoes, onions, dried fish, pulses, frozen seafood, frog legs |
| Belgium | spices, dehydrated vegetables, deep-frozen food |
| Brazil | spices, dehydrated vegetables |
| Canada | spices, potatoes, onions |
| Chile | spices, dehydrated vegetables, onions, potatoes, chicken |
| China | potatoes, garlic, apples, spices, onions, Chinese sausage, Chinese wine |
| Cuba | potatoes, onions, cocoa beans |
| Denmark | spices |
| Finland | spices |
| France | spices, vegetable seasonings, frozen and deboned chicken |
| Hungary | spices, onion, wine cork |

*(continues)*

◁  **WORLDWIDE APPROVED USES OF**
   **IRRADIATED FOODS** *(continued)*  ▷

| COUNTRY | FOOD PRODUCT(S) |
|---|---|
| Indonesia | spices, tuber and root crops |
| Israel | spices, potatoes, onions, grains |
| Japan | potatoes |
| Korea | garllc powder, potatoes, onions, spices, frozen products, poultry, dehydrated vegetables, rice, egg powder, packaging materials |
| Norway | spices |
| Pakistan | potatoes, onions, garlic, spices |
| Russia | potatoes, onions, cereals, fresh and dried fruits and vegetables, meat and meat products, poultry, grains |
| South Africa | potatoes, onions, fruit, spices, meat, fish, processed chicken products, vegetables |
| Spain | potatoes, onions |
| Syria | potatoes, onions, chicken, fruit, spices |
| Thailand | onions, fermented pork sausages, potatoes |

Source: Adapted from S. M. Tando Jam, "Radioisotope—A Tool for Agriculture Sciences," *Pakistan Economist*. Available online. URL: http://www.pakistaneconomist.com/issue2002/issue32/i&e7.htm.

molecules and DNA molecules, causes that organism to die, ensuring that it no longer poses a threat to the food in which it occurs. Irradiation is able to destroy these critical molecules because radiation that strikes a substance transfers some of its energy to electrons in the substance. As those electrons gain energy, they tend to move about more rapidly. If an electron that is part of a chemical bond is affected in this way, it may break loose from the bond, causing the bond itself to break. And if that bond is part of a protein molecule, a molecule of nucleic acid, or some other critical molecule, that molecule breaks apart and is no longer able to carry out its normal functions. In such a case, the organism in which that molecule exists (such as a pathogen) may become ill and die, thus losing its ability to cause decay in the food it inhabits. The breaking of chemical bonds by radiation of any type is known as *radiolysis,* and the new substances formed as a result of the process (the fragments of the original molecule) are known as *radiolytic products.*

Three methods are used for the irradiation of foods. They make use of (1) radionuclides, (2) electron beams (e-beams), and (3) X-rays.

Radionuclides are radioactive isotopes that decay with the emission of some form of radiation: alpha, beta, or gamma rays. Cobalt-60 is the most common radionuclide used in food irradiation. (A second radionuclide, cesium-137, is also used for the irradiation of foods, but rarely.) Cobalt-60 decays to produce nickel-60 with a half-life of about 5.3 years; the half-life of a radioactive isotope is the time required for one half of a sample of the isotope to decay. The products of this decay are nickel-60, which is not radioactive; beta particles ($_{-1}^{0}e$; electrons); and gamma rays ($\gamma$; high-energy forms of electromagnetic radiation):

$$_{27}^{60}Co \rightarrow {}_{28}^{60}Ni + -_{1}^{0}e + \gamma$$

Cobalt-60 is produced from stable (nonradioactive) cobalt-59 at a processing facility and then plated with a nickel coating and deposited in a zirconium case. The cobalt-nickel-zirconium aggregate is then enclosed in thin cylindrical containers ("pencils") about 18 inches long for shipment to a irradiation facility. When not in use, the cobalt-60 pencils are stored underwater to protect workers and the surrounding environment from radiation. A food product to be irradiated is placed on a conveyor belt and passed beneath an array of cobalt-60 pencils. The gamma rays emitted from the isotope destroy pathogens that may be present in the food.

Food irradiation with cobalt-60 has a number of advantages. The gamma rays produced during decay of the radionuclide penetrate deeply and uniformly through the foods at which they are directed, guaranteeing a complete and efficient treatment. The only decay product formed when cobalt-60 is used is nickel-60, which is not radioactive and can be safely recovered and reused. There are essentially no drawbacks to the use of cobalt-60, either in terms of possible health effects to humans or environmental harm. The major drawback of the process, from an industrial standpoint, is that it tends to proceed relatively slowly and does require the replacement of cobalt-60 pencils about every 15 years or so.

In the second method of irradiation, electron beams are generated in a linear accelerator. (A linear accelerator is a device for accelerating protons, electrons, and other fundamental particles to very high rates of speed, usually about 99 percent the speed of light.) When an electron beam comes into contact with food, it destroys pathogens that are responsible for food-borne illnesses. Electron-beam (or e-beam) systems have an advantage over cobalt-60 systems in that they can be turned on and off, whereas radioactive isotopes produce radiation continuously and must be stored in protected areas when they are not actually in use. E-beam systems also avoid concerns that some people have about the use of radioactive materials to irradiate foods, because such materials have no part in e-beam technology. One disadvantage of e-beam systems, however, is that electron beams do not penetrate as deeply into foods as the radiation from radionuclides. If deep penetration is needed, the e-beams must first be converted to X-rays. Also, e-beam systems tend to be more complex and more expensive to operate than are radionucleotide-based systems.

X-ray systems operate on essentially the same principle as e-beam systems. The difference is that electron beams generated in an accelerator are made to collide with a metal plate, converting some portion of the electron beams into more energetic X-rays. These X-rays can then be directed at the food product that is to irradiated. X-ray systems obviously have some of the same disadvantages of e-beam systems (complexity and cost), but, like radionucleotide systems, they are able to penetrate food products to a greater depth and more efficiently than electron-beam systems.

## The Irradiation Controversy

The practice of irradiating foods has aroused significant debate between proponents and skeptics. The subjects of debate relate to the actual effect of radiation on pathogens, the chemical changes that irradiation produces in food, the environmental effects of irradiation practices, and the nutritional value of irradiated foods.

Proponents of food irradiation point out that radiation is an extremely effective means of killing up to 99.9 percent of the pathogens that cause millions of cases of food-borne illness and thousands of deaths each year in the United States. The process is also useful in agricultural situations, such as deinfesting grains and flours, because it leaves behind no harmful chemical residues. Opponents argue that the long-term use of radiation on foods is harmful because, as is the case with pesticides, only the hardiest pests survive and these survivors eventually develop into pathogen strains that are even more resistant to radiation. Also, because radiation can be used on only certain foods, irradiating foods can address only a limited part of the nation's food-borne-illness problem.

Opponents argue that scientific information about the effects of radiation on foods themselves, distinct from the pathogens they may harbor, is too scarce. That is, if radiation can break chemical bonds and produce radiolytic products in pathogens, can it not have the same effect in foods? Among the most common radiolytic products are chemical species known as free radicals that have been implicated in the development of cancers. Opponents ask, might not food irradiation lead to an increase in cancer cases as a result of the free radicals formed in the process? Is it not possible, they say, that irradiated foods may eventually result in leukemia, other forms of cancer, and kidney disease? The risk might be, then, that irradiation of food would result in an increase in certain diseases, such as cancer.

Proponents of irradiation point out that a number of studies of irradiated food have been conducted, and thus far no evidence has been reported that such foods are harmful in any way to consumers. In a 1998 report on this issue, Dr. Kim M. Morehouse, a research chemist at the FDA's Center for Food Safety and Applied Nutrition summarized the findings of the World Health Organization (WHO), the Food and Agricultural Organization (FAO) of the United Nations (FAO), the Codex Alimentarius Commission, and the FDA on the safety of irradiated foods: "These organizations have all concluded that food irradiation is safe when Good Manufacturing Practices (GMPs) and Good Irradiation Practices are used."

Proponents of food irradiation suggest that radioactive materials used in food irradiation are packaged, used, and disposed of with a high level of security and that there is no record of any person ever having been exposed to dangerous radiation at any food irradiation facility. Opponents tend to express a common general concern among many Americans that almost anything having to do with radioactivity poses a potential risk to the public and that the nation's food supply should not be exposed to radiation that makes harmful changes in those foods. The idea that foods exposed to radiation will become radioactive themselves appears to have no scientific foundation.

Those who oppose the irradiation of foods are concerned that the practice may destroy important nutritional substances, such as vitamins and minerals, resulting in foods that are less nutritious than they should be. They claim that radiation may be especially harmful to vitamins A, C, and E; the B complex vitamins; and beta-carotene. Proponents of food irradiation respond to such statements by pointing to large numbers of studies that have been conducted on the effects of radiation on the nutritional properties of food. They tend to take essentially the same position: Irradiated foods are as nutritious as foods that have not been treated by radiation. On its "Frequently Asked Questions about Food Irradiation," for example, the Centers for Disease Control and Prevention states: "An overwhelming body of scientific evidence demonstrates that irradiation does not harm the nutritional value of food, nor does it make the food unsafe to eat."

# Public Opinion on Irradiated Foods

The debate over irradiated foods has thus far involved relatively small numbers of people, primarily those with a vested interest in the use of radiation technologies and consumer groups with strong feelings about food irradiation. Public opinion polls tend to show that less than half of the general public is informed about the subject. But if food irradiation is to be adopted in the United States and other nations, the general public must be willing to buy and eat irradiated foods. How does the public feel about irradiated foods? A number of studies have been conducted to answer this question.

At first glance, those studies appear to show that a large majority of Americans would not buy and eat irradiated foods. A 1997 CBS News poll, for example, found that 77 percent of respondents would not buy irradiated foods. A poll conducted by the Food Marketing Institute produced even more dramatic results. The study found that the percentage of consumers who said they would buy irradiated foods dropped from 79 percent in 1998 to 38 percent in 2000.

An important factor in such polling, however, is the extent to which respondents are familiar with irradiated foods. Other studies suggest that the more consumers know about irradiated foods, the more likely they are to buy and eat those foods. When consumers in Georgia were offered to try irradiated foods in a 2003 study, for example, researchers found that acceptance of such foods increased from 29 percent in a 1993 study (when they did not try irradiated foods) to 69 percent in 2003 (when they did). The Georgia study cited earlier research that reported similar results. Researchers concluded that, in general, the more people know about irradiated foods, the more favorable they are of purchasing and consuming such foods and the more willing they are to pay a premium for irradiated foods.

The one point about which almost everyone agrees today is that irradiated foods should carry some type of label so that consumers know in advance what they are buying. The current U.S. regulations dealing with irradiation labeling are a bit inconsistent. Any food that has been irradiated must carry the radura logo and a verbal statement such as "treated with radiation" or "treated by radiation." That labeling is required, however, only on foods sold to a first buyer. For example, if potatoes treated with radiation are sold to a company that makes potato chips, the potatoes must be labeled when sold to the company, but the potato chips do not have to indicate that the potatoes from which they were made were irradiated. The radiation of spices is one of the largest applications of food irradiation today. Because of current labeling practices, however, foods made with irradiated spices carry no label indicating that they have been treated with radiation.

Labeling of irradiated foods is in a period of transition. In 2002, Congress passed the Farm Security and Investment Act, which, among other provisions, directed the FDA to revise its regulations on the labeling of irradiated food products to make them somewhat less restrictive. As a result, the FDA began to allow use of the phrase "cold pasteurization" in place of "irradiation" in 2003. As one might expect, consumer groups objected to this decision, arguing that the change was simply a way to allow the food industry to continue using an objectionable and possibly risky practice without notifying consumers. The labeling of irradiated food, as with so many other practices that are changing the way in which foods are produced, delivered, and sold in the United States and other countries of the world, is likely to remain a contentious issue for years to come.

# 6
# ORGANIC AND
# NATURAL FOODS

The last few decades of the 20th century saw a rapidly growing interest in foods labeled as "natural," "organic," "whole," "healthful," or some similar descriptive term. The precise meaning of those terms has often been difficult to determine, and the difference among them equally as hard to distinguish. Some individuals and businesses have attempted to clarify what they mean when they use each of these terms. For example, the University of Iowa Health Care program has defined a *health food* as "any food that contributes to overall improved health status." The program points out that the term should be used for foods that are known to benefit human health—such as fruits, vegetables, whole grains, beans, cereals, low-fat milk and dairy products, and lean meats and poultry—rather than products that are simply *labeled* as "health foods." The Food Marketing Institute defines natural foods as "foods that are minimally processed and free of artificial color, flavors, preservatives, and additives." But it points out that the term can be misleading since there are no governmental controls on the use of the word natural for foods and, at least in theory, any company or individual can use the term on any food product that it offers for sale.

The only term for which a clear and specific definition exists is that of *organic foods*. In 1990, Congress passed the Organic Foods Production

Producers can label these free-range egg-laying chickens as "wholesome," "natural," or "whole" foods, but they can call them "organic" only if they meet certain USDA standards. (Nigel Cattlin/Photo Researchers, Inc.)

Act (OFPA) to set national standards governing the marketing of so-called organically produced products, to assure consumers that organically produced products meet a consistent standard; and to facilitate interstate commerce in fresh and processed food that is organically produced. The OFPA established the National Organic Program (NOP) within the U.S. Department of Agriculture (USDA) and ordered the department to establish standards for defining foods that could be labeled as *organic* in the United States. The NOP promulgated those standards on October 21, 2002. They defined organic food as follows:

Organic food is produced by farmers who emphasize the use of renewable resources and the conservation of soil and water to enhance environmental quality for future generations. Organic meat, poultry, eggs, and dairy products come from animals that are given no antibiotics or growth hormones. Organic food is produced without using most conventional pesticides; fertilizers made with synthetic ingredients or sewage sludge; bioengineering; or ionizing radiation.

(Source: "Organic Food Standards and Labels: The Facts."
Available online. URL: http://www.ams.usda.gov/nop/
Consumers/brochure.html)

A critical point to be noted about this definition is that it refers to the *methods* by which a food is produced; it does not describe the actual food itself.

The OFPA and its administrative rules provide an exhaustive list of materials and procedures that are permitted and prohibited in the production, storage, shipping, and sale of foods that can be legally labeled as *organic*. The USDA's "National List of Allowed and Prohibited Substances," for example, lists dozens of synthetic products that *may* be used in the production of organic foods (such as alcohols, calcium hypochlorite, chlorine dioxide, hydrogen peroxide, soap-based herbicides, plastic mulches, sulfur, insecticidal soaps, copper sulfate, ethylene, lignin sulfonate, and sodium silicate) and others that *may not* be used in the production of organic foods (such as ash from manure burning, arsenic, lead salts, sodium fluoaluminate, strychnine, tobacco dust [nicotine sulfate], potassium chloride [in most cases], and sodium nitrate).

Food products that meet the USDA's standards may be marked (but are not required to be) with a distinctive package label. The label indicates that at least 95 percent of the food in the package has been produced by methods approved by the USDA. It can be used, however, only with single-ingredient foods, such as meats, milk, eggs, cereals, and cheese. Multiple-ingredient foods that contain at least 70 percent organic ingredients cannot carry the USDA seal, but it can carry the statement "made with organic ingredients." Finally, food products that contain less than 70 percent organic foods cannot carry either the USDA label or the "made with organic ingredients" notice, although they can list organically produced ingredients on the side panel.

Food producers have reason to use terms such as *natural, healthful, whole,* and *organic* in describing their products. Public opinion surveys show that a majority of Americans prefer to purchase foods that contain fewer pesticides, are environmentally friendly, and are more nutritious. They are likely to associate *natural, healthful, whole,* and *organic* foods with these characteristics. Yet, except for the term *organic,* no standards exist to define other types of "healthful" foods. Absent those standards, consumers have no guarantee that the foods they believe to be safe and nutritious actually have those qualities. This problem becomes ever more important as interest in healthful foods among consumers grows.

## Growing Interest in Natural and Organic Foods

Interest in natural and organic foods can be traced only as far back as the 1940s. Before then, nearly all foods available for sale could probably be described as "natural" or "organic," in that they were shipped almost directly from the farm or dairy to the marketplace. In 1920, for example, one in three Americans lived on farms. In most cases, their diets consisted of foods grown on their own property or purchased from neighbors. Only 50 years later, fewer than one in 20 Americans lived on farms. Most people purchased their groceries at stores, where products were canned, frozen, dried, or otherwise preserved.

The revolution in modern food processing can be traced to the years after World War II when a host of new processing technologies were developed. By the 1950s and 1960s, hundreds of new food products made by these technologies were available to consumers and the proportion of direct-from-the-farm products decreased significantly. In response to this trend, a relatively small number of consumers began to express concerns about the effects of food processing on the aesthetic and nutritional qualities of the food products being made available to Americans. In a number of locations, stores specializing in "natural" and "organic" foods began to open. Sales at these stores

# ◄ LADY EVE BALFOUR (1898–1990) ►

*The attitude of the organic farmer, who has trained himself to think ecologically, is different [from that of the 'modern conventional farmer']. He tries to see the living world as a whole. He regards so-called pests and weeds as part of the natural pattern of the Biota, probably necessary to its stability and permanence, to be utilized rather than attacked. Throughout his operations he endeavours to achieve his objective by co-operating with natural agencies in place of relying on man-made substitutes. He studies what appear to be nature's rules—as manifested in a healthy wilderness—and attempts to adapt them to his own farm needs, instead of flouting them.*
—Lady Eve Balfour, "Towards a Sustainable
Agriculture—The Living Soil," an address given at
the International Federation of Organic Agriculture
Movements, Sissach, Switzerland, 1977.

The post–World War II world saw a collision between two sharply contrasting views of agriculture. One was a traditional, "organic" approach focused on the growth of crops and livestock that made use primarily of natural materials. The other was a newer, more "modern" approach that relied on the extensive use of synthetic chemicals for fertilizers and pesticides. For most of the last half of the 20th century, it appeared that the latter view would win out. Yet, a strong movement continued to call for reliance on natural fertilizers and pest-control systems. One of the strongest and most persistent voices for that philosophy was Lady Eve Balfour.

Eve Balfour was born in London on July 16, 1898. Her family boasted a number of famous names, including her great-grandfather, Bulwer Lytton, who was a poet, critic, novelist, and politician; an uncle, John William Strutt, Lord Rayleigh, the winner of the 1904 Nobel Prize in physics; and another uncle, A. J. Balfour, who served as Prime Minister of Great Britain from 1901 to 1905. Eve Balfour grew up in an extended family of one brother, four sisters, and a number of cousins that included overall eight girls and three boys. The family divided its time between two households, one in Woking, Surrey, and the other in Whittingehame, East Lothia. The family group was apparently a somewhat unusual one for the time, one in which children's ideas and interests were taken seriously. Eve's natural interests in a host of subjects, therefore, bloomed early with the encouragement of her parents, aunts, and uncles.

Eve developed a serious interest in nature early in life, declaring at the age of 12 that she had decided to become a farmer. In spite of the unusual request from a member of the upper class, Eve's parents offered their support immediately. They provided her with a private tutor to help her prepare for a career in agriculture, and arranged for her to be enrolled at the Reading University College Agricultural Department when she was old enough to be admitted. In 1915, Eve began her course of study at Reading and two years later was awarded her Farming Diploma. Afterward she was hired to supervise a 50-acre farm operated by the Women's War Agricultural Committee in Monmouthshire, near Rogerstone.

Given the pressures of World War I, Balfour's experience at Monmouthshire was a challenging and difficult one, but it only confirmed her desire to remain in agriculture. After the war, in 1919, she and her sister Mary purchased a 157-acre farm at Haughley in Suffolk, called New Bells. Eve remained at New Bells for most of the remaining years of her life, for much of the time with Mary at her side, along with two women companions, Beb Hearnden and Kathleen Carnley ("K.C."), her domestic partner of 50 years.

Besides operating the New Bells farm, Balfour also pursued a number of other activities, which ranged from organizing a dance band and writing detective novels to earning a pilot's license and participating in the Tithe War, a movement to relieve farmers of the 10 percent tax they had traditionally been charged by landowners in England. In spite of these activities, Balfour's primary focus throughout her life was on organic approaches to agriculture. She wrote about her philosophy in some detail in her most famous book, *The Living Soil,* first published in 1943. The book explained the scientific basis for organic agriculture and outlined the extensive research program that had been undertaken at Haughley, comparing three approaches to farming: organic, conventional (involving the use of chemical fertilizers and pesticides), and "mixed" (combining elements of both organic and conventional approaches). *The Living Soil* went through a number of editions and is still regarded as the "bible" of the modern organic movement.

In 1945, Balfour was one of the founding members of the Soil Association, an organization founded on the principle that the key to healthy humans is healthy soil, which, in turn, is made possible by the use of organic farming techniques, such as crop rotation, and the avoidance of synthetic chemicals. Today, the association calls itself the United Kingdom's "leading campaigning

*(continues)*

---

**(continued)**

and certification organisation for organic food and farming." Balfour remained active in the Soil Association until the last years of her life, often acting as its most public spokesperson and its reminder of the reasons for which the organization was created. She continued to write and speak about her passion for organic farming into the tenth decade of her life, and in 1990 she was (somewhat belatedly) awarded an O.B.E. in the New Year's Honours List. Only two weeks later, on January 14, 1990, she died at her home in Theberton.

---

represented only a very small fraction (about 1 percent) of all food sales in the nation, however. Many people regarded such stores as the province of individuals with somewhat "peculiar" eating habits.

As late as 1990 the sale of natural and organic foods was still largely restricted to two minor sources: specialized natural food stores and direct sales from producers, such as at farmers markets. In 1991, 68 percent of all natural and organic foods were sold through specialized natural food stores, about 25 percent directly from producers, and only 7 percent through conventional food markets. But the early 1990s saw a sudden and dramatic change in the role of natural and organic foods in the American diet. Such products suddenly became of interest to a much broader audience of Americans, as recorded by the Department of Agriculture's Economic Research Service (ERS) and the Food Marketing Institute. As the graph on page 181 shows, the sale of organic fruits and vegetables increased from less than $181 million in 1990 to $2.2 billion in 2000. During the same period, total sales of organic milk (first made available in conventional supermarkets in 1993) jumped from $15.8 million in 1996 to $104 million in 2000. Overall, sales of natural and organic food products have been increasing at a rate of more than 20 percent annually since the mid-1990s, reaching a total of $8.5 billion in 2002, the last year for which data are available.

Conventional food stores noticed this change in consumer spending patterns and began to stock natural and organic foods. Between 1995

## ◁ SIR ALBERT HOWARD (1873–1947) ▷

When one reads today about the beginnings of organic farming, mention is often made of the great changes that took place after World War II, as a few individuals opposed the rapid introduction of synthetic fertilizers and pesticides into agricultural programs and argued, instead, for a "return to basics" in farming and dairying methods. But organic farming is hardly a new concept. Farmers throughout the world have known about and practiced organic farming techniques for thousands of years. Historians of the organic farming movement sometimes point to the work of Sir Albert Howard in rediscovering and testing scientifically organic farming techniques that had been used by the Chinese for at least 4,000 years.

Albert Howard was born on December 8, 1873, at Bishop's Castle, Shropshire, son to Richard Howard and Ann Kilvert Howard. He attended Wrekin College, an independent boarding school in Shropshire, before matriculating at the Royal College of Science, in South Kensington, London. He then received an appointment as Foundation Scholar at St. John's College, Cambridge, where he earned First Class Natural Sciences Tripos (final examinations in a subject) in 1896 and 1897 and was awarded a Cambridge Diploma of Agriculture and National Diploma of Agriculture in 1899. In the same year, he was appointed Lecturer in Agricultural Science at Harrison College in the Barbados and Mycologist and Agricultural Lecturer at the Imperial Department of Agriculture for the West Indies. In 1903, he returned to England, where he took a position as botanist at the Southeastern Agricultural College in Wye. Two years later, he left Wye to become Imperial Economic Botanist to the Government of India.

Howard served as an agricultural adviser for the British government in India from 1905 to 1931. During his period of service, Howard witnessed the introduction of some early scientific agricultural techniques to Indian farmers, techniques that involved the use of synthetic fertilizers and pesticides. Howard noted that such techniques sometimes seemed to be less successful than more traditional techniques about which he had learned. An important influence in his own interest in traditional farming techniques was a book by the American missionary F. H. King, *The Farmers of Forty Centuries*, that told of practices traditionally followed by Chinese farmers.

*(continues)*

*(continued)*

Howard decided to carry out experiments to determine those practices that were most likely to improve the growth of traditional Indian crops. He was especially interested in learning more about the best method by which materials could be composted, allowing waste products to be returned to the soil for more productive farming. He experimented with a variety of different materials, both natural and synthetic, and different methods of treating those materials that resulted in the richest form of compost. The most efficient system he discovered is one that would be familiar to many modern-day organic farmers. It involved stacking alternate layers of animal manure, sewage sludge, garbage, straw, and leaves that were turned occasionally over a period of six months or longer. Liquids drained from the decomposing materials were then recycled to maintain adequate moisture in the piles. The method is sometimes referred to as the "Indore process," named after the Indian state in which Howard was working at the time.

Howard's research extended far beyond the development of more efficient composting techniques, however. His experiments were inspired by a simple philosophy that all aspects of nature—soil, crops, livestock, and humans—were part of a natural whole and that agricultural procedures that treated any single element in isolation from the others were doomed to be less successful than they could be. Howard summarized his quarter-century of research in India and his philosophy of what would now be called organic farming in *An Agricultural Testament,* a book published in 1943 that is still a bible to many organic farmers.

After his return to England in 1931, Howard was active in the organic farming movement that was just developing in that nation. He strongly influenced the work of other early organic farming enthusiasts, including J. I. Rodale and Lady Eve Balfour. Both were founders of England's Soil Association, the nation's best-known group working for the improvement of organic farming technique and for the dissemination of information about such techniques.

During his lifetime, Howard received a number of honors, including the Silver Medal of the Royal Society of Arts in 1920 and the Barclay Memorial Medal of the Royal Asiatic Society of Bengal in 1930. He was made a Fellow of that society in 1928 and an Honorary Fellow of the Imperial College of Science in 1935. He was knighted in 1934. Howard died on October 20, 1947, at Blackheath, London.

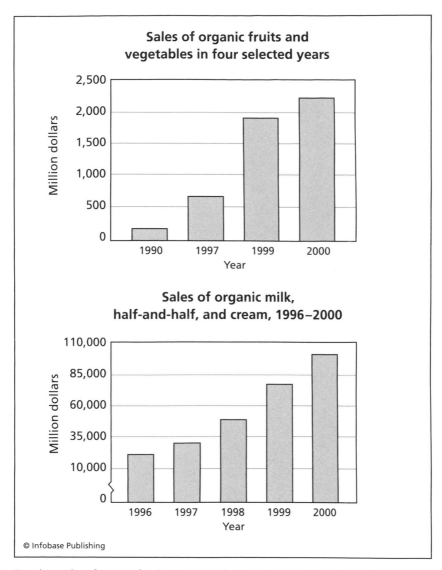

Trends in sales of organic foods: (a) organic fruits and vegetables in four selected years; (b) organic milk, half-and-half, and cream, 1996–2000

and 2000, the percentage of natural and organic foods sold in conventional markets jumped from less than 10 percent to more than 50 percent. The Food Marketing Institute estimates that organic foods are now available at more than 20,000 natural food stores and more than 75 percent of all conventional markets.

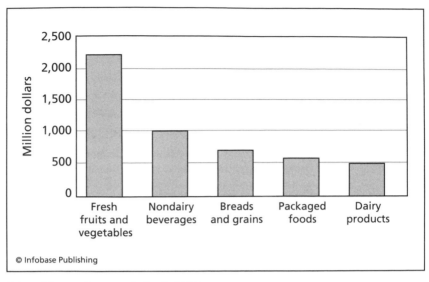

Sales of the top five organic foods, 2000

Today, a wide variety of natural and organic food products are commercially available. By far the most popular are fresh fruits and vegetables, with sales of about $2.2 billion, followed by nondairy beverages, breads and grains, dairy products, and packaged foods (which includes frozen and dried prepared foods, baby food, soups, and desserts). The graph above shows the five top-selling types of natural foods in the United States in 2000.

## The Costs of Organic Foods

One of the intriguing features of the natural and organic food movement is that such foods tend to cost significantly more than their conventional counterparts. A number of studies have been conducted on the premium that consumers pay for natural and organic foods. For example, the ERS reported on a study of produce sold at the Boston wholesale market during the 2000–2001 season in which the cost of organic broccoli was 30 percent higher on average than the conventional product; the cost of organic carrots was 25 percent higher; and the cost of organic mesclun was 10 percent higher. Studies routinely show that the price of such foods ranges from 10 to 250 percent more than for comparable foods from conventional sources. The results of one such study are shown in the graph on page 184.

How is it possible to explain the additional costs of producing organic foods compared to their conventional counterparts? The answer that organic farmers give is that they have additional costs that are not part of the process of raising conventional crops and animals. For instance:

➢ Labor costs tend to be much higher on organic farms because of the labor-intensive agricultural practices used, such as hand-weeding, hand-tilling, composting, and crop rotation.

➢ The cost of natural fertilizers tends to be significantly greater than that of synthetic fertilizers.

Organic farming excludes the use of chemicals such as weed killers and insecticides. (Mauro Fermariello/Photo Researchers, Inc.)

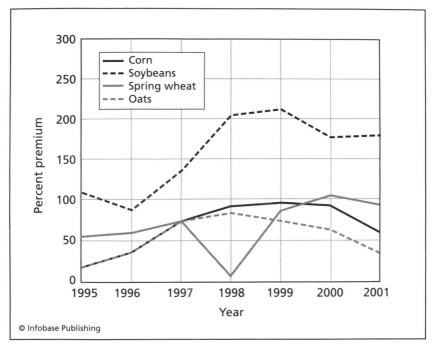

Price premiums paid for organic frozen vegetables, 1995–2001

➤ Organic farmers tend to experience a significantly greater amount of crop loss than do conventional farmers because the former do not use chemicals to reduce spoilage (such as pesticides and fungicides). According to some studies, the yield for an organically grown crop may be anywhere from 10 to 40 percent less than that for a conventionally grown crop of the same kind.

➤ The relatively small size of organic farms compared with conventional farms means that the per-unit cost of a farm product is likely to be greater.

➤ Organic foods still tend to represent a relatively small percentage of the overall food market, with the result that large, cost-effective storage and transportation systems are still not well developed.

➤ The adoption of the Organic Foods Production Act of 1990, while a boon to consumers, resulted in additional costs to farmers who wish to meet its stringent requirements and have their products legally certified as "organic."

Proponents of organic farming also like to point out that their practices provide a number of hidden benefits which, in effect, reduce the real overall price of the products. For example, they claim that organic farming and animal practices

➤ protect and improve the environment, reducing future costs needed to deal with pollution and land degradation;

➤ maintain higher standards for domestic animals, reducing the costs of caring for sick animals;

➤ reduce farm laborers' exposure to potentially toxic pesticides and synthetic fertilizers, reducing the health costs for those employees;

➤ contribute to the development of rural areas by generating additional farm employment and increasing income in local communities.

Organic proponents say that the problem is not that organic food is too expensive, but that conventional foods are unrealistically inexpensive. That is, the practices by which they are grown tend to have hidden costs that society as a whole eventually has to pay and that should be factored into the real costs of conventional foods. However sound these arguments may or may not be, consumers in the United States and other countries appear to be willing, in increasingly large numbers, to pay the additional cost for organic foods.

## Organic Foods: The Consumer Rationale

It seems clear that Americans have become convinced that they should include more natural and organic foods in their diets. What is it about these products that makes consumers willing to pay more—often significantly more—than their conventional counterparts? For a number of years, proponents of organic foods have been suggesting a number of benefits to be gained from including more organic and natural foods in one's diet. They offer four main assertions: that organic foods have more aesthetic appeal; that they are safer to eat than processed foods; that they contribute to better human health; and that they benefit the environment.

As an example of the first claim, an article in *National Grocer Magazine* claims that the taste and appearance of natural and conventional products are often different. "For example, the article claims, "natural peanut butter tastes like peanuts, rather than a peanut-based sandwich spread. A sip of a natural peach juice will be more reminiscent of biting into a fresh peach than a commercial juice whose added sweeteners and artificial flavors will be more closely aligned to a fruit punch than fresh fruit." Other proponents use terms like *more flavorful, fresher, better tasting,* and *more vivid* when describing organic foods. The claim is also made that professional chefs prefer organic foods. In one survey conducted by *Food and Wine* magazine in 1997, 76 percent of chefs questioned said they "actively seek out organically grown ingredients."

One problem with the argument that organic foods taste better is that it tends to be based on anecdotal reports that are not necessarily supported by scientific research. A number of studies have been conducted in which consumers have been offered organic and nonorganic versions of the same product and asked which had the better taste. In virtually every case, consumers have been unable to distinguish the taste between the two types of food. In 2003, for example, the Good Housekeeping Institute conducted a blind tasting of organic and nonorganic versions of three food products, organic Cascadian Farms' Honey Nut O's with General Mills' Honey Nut Cheerios (both made by the same company); Heinz Organic Ketchup with Heinz Ketchup, and Country Choice Vanilla Sandwich Cremes with Nabisco's Oreos. The results of this test showed that people generally found no difference in taste between the organic and nonorganic versions of the foods.

One factor that affects the results of taste tests appears to be whether or not consumers are aware of which kinds of foods they are tasting. In one notable case in Great Britain, the large supermarket chain Tesco conducted a number of in-store taste tests that seemed to indicate that people preferred the taste of organic to nonorganic foods. The company's claims, however, were challenged by the British Advertising Standards Authority, which conducted tests of its own. The Authority discovered that in blind taste tests, where people did not know which kind of food they were tasting, they found essentially no differences in taste between organic and nonorganic foods.

Interestingly enough, some taste tests appear to suggest that at least some people prefer the taste of nonorganic to organic foods. In 1999, for example, a student at Berkeley High School in California conducted an informal taste test of organic foods among fourth and fifth graders in the city's elementary schools. He found that students generally tended to prefer processed foods to their organic counterparts. He explained his results by suggesting that "kids have been eating sugar and fast food for so long, they just don't like the taste of organic. They've never had it before, so it tastes strange to them."

One of the strongest arguments presented by organic food enthusiasts is that such foods are safer to consume because they are grown without the use of the synthetic chemicals found in pesticides or chemical fertilizers (neither of which may be used in the production of organic foods). There is certainly some evidence to support the view that organic foods are safer. The Consumers Union, which publishes *Consumer Reports,* one of the most highly respected consumer magazines in the nation, has conducted tests and reviews of research on the relative amounts of pesticides found on organic and nonorganic food products. They have found consistently that organic foods have lower amounts of pesticides, approaching zero in many instances, compared to conventionally produced foods. In 2002, for example, the magazine reported that pesticide residues were found on 95 percent of all pears produced by conventional methods, compared with 25 percent produced organically. Similar differences were noted for peaches (93 percent to 50 percent), sweet bell peppers (69 percent to 9 percent), strawberries (91 percent to 25 percent), spinach (84 percent to 47 percent), and other fruits and vegetables.

In spite of these findings, most authorities in the field of food science are reluctant to acknowledge any clear-cut benefits of eating organic foods rather than their processed counterparts. Disinterested organizations and individuals frequently express the position that there is no significant scientific evidence that organic foods are, in general, safer than nonorganic foods. They tend to point out that very few controlled scientific studies have been conducted on the relative safety of the two types of food, and those studies that have been completed tend to show little or no differences. For example, C. M. Williams, in the Hugh Sinclair Unit of Human Nutrition of the School of Food Biosciences at the University of Reading in the United Kingdom, completed an exhaustive review of studies on the nutritional value of organic foods in 2002. He concluded the following: "There appears to be widespread perception amongst consumers that such [organic] methods result in foods of higher nutritional quality. The present review concludes that evidence that can support or refute such perception is not available in the scientific literature."

Proponents of organic foods often argue that such foods are not only safer than processed foods, they are also healthier. That is, by eating organic rather than processed foods, a person can achieve a healthier lifestyle with less disease and, presumably, a longer life—according to the assertion. Over the years, a number of specific claims have been made for a variety of organic foods. For example, the Holistic Health Tools Web site encourages the use of green tea because it has a number of health benefits, including prevention of cancer; reduction in cholesterol levels, blood pressure, and blood sugar levels; and antibacterial and antiviral actions. At times, proponents for the health benefits of organic foods carry their claims to the extreme. A Web site on the health benefits of flaxseed, for example, claims that the product may protect a person against heart disease, elevated cholesterol, hypertension, high blood pressure, diabetes, certain types of cancers, rheumatoid arthritis, lupus, eczema, psoriasis, skin problems, side effects of menopause and osteoporosis, ulcerative colitis, diverticulitis, constipation, multiple sclerosis, endometriosis, hair loss, insomnia, and attention deficit disorder (ADD).

As with claims for the safety of organic foods, claims for their health benefits often rely on anecdotal reports and folk beliefs. Neither necessarily invalidates such claims, but they are not the same as scientific confirmation. In recent years, some researchers have carried out controlled experiments to determine the extent to which such claims may be valid. The results of such studies are now beginning to accumulate, providing at least some minimal support for the health claims made for at least some organic foods.

For example, Dr. Virginia Worthington, at Johns Hopkins University, reported in 2001 on a review of 41 published studies comparing the nutritional value of organically and conventionally grown fruits, vegetables, and grains. She found that the organic products tended to have higher concentrations of vitamins C (27 percent more than in conventionally grown foods), iron (21.1 percent more), magnesium (29.3 percent more), and phosphorus (13.6 percent more). Worthington concluded that five servings of organic vegetables provided the recommended daily intake of vitamin C for men and women, while comparable amounts of conventional counterparts did not. The special benefits of vitamin C provided by organic foods have been noted by other researchers as well. For example, Theo Clark, professor of chemistry at Truman State University in Missouri, reported in 2002 that organically grown oranges have as much as 30 percent more vitamin C as their conventionally grown counterparts, as did an extensive study conducted under the auspices of the Soil Association of the United Kingdom, reported in 2001. The U.K. study also found that organic crops tend to have contain higher concentrations of essential minerals and phytonutrients. Phytonutrients are chemicals derived from plants, such as beta carotene, capsaicin, and flavonoids, that benefit human health.

Research sometimes focuses on very specific health benefits provided by certain types of organic foods. In 2003, for example, Alyson Mitchell, assistant professor of food science at the University of California at Davis, reported that three organic food products—corn, strawberries, and marionberries—had significantly higher concentrations of compounds known as polyphenolics, natural antioxidants that occur in plants, than their conventional counterparts. They may protect against a variety of diseases and disorders, such as heart attack, stroke, hardening of the arteries, Alzheimer's disease, diabetes, certain eye diseases, arthritis, and osteoporosis, as well as reducing the normal process of ageing. These compounds are produced naturally by all plants as a way of combating attacks by insect predators. But they appear to be largely destroyed by pesticides used on conventional crops. When pesticides are *not* used, foods retain the polyphenolics and are available to people who eat the pesticide-free foods.

In spite of such research supporting the health benefits of organic foods, many authorities are still wary about promoting health claims too vigorously. Most governmental agencies still take a cautious stance, suggesting that the nutritional value of organic and conventional foods are essentially equivalent. Perhaps of greatest significance, the U.S. Department of Agriculture makes no claims that organic food is healthier (or safer or tastier or more attractive or superior in any other way) than conventional foods.

Finally, proponents of organic food suggest that the farming techniques by which such foods are grown tend to have a favorable impact on the environment. A report on organic farming presented to the Scottish parliament in 2002 identified seven general categories of claimed benefits:

> ➤ Biodiversity protection: Because synthetic pesticides, fertilizers, and other nonnatural chemicals are used in the farming process, there is likely to be a reduced impact on plants and animals living in the area where crops are being produced.

> ➤ Soil health: Organic farming may have positive effects on the soil, again because synthetic chemicals are avoided, and also because traditional soil improvement techniques, such as crop rotation and composting, are routinely incorporated in organic farming procedures. Because synthetic pesticides are not used, helpful macro- and microorganisms in the soil, such as worms and bacteria, are not destroyed and contribute to the enrichment of the soil used in farming.

> ➤ Water retention of soil: Manipulation of the soil, an essential process used in organic farming, also tends to improve the soil's ability to hold water and control its flow through the soil, reducing erosion that is sometimes associated with conventional farming.

> ➤ Reduction of greenhouse gases: Organic farming, according to some proponents, may reduce the amount of carbon dioxide, am-

monia, and methane released to the atmosphere, thereby contributing to the reduction in greenhouse emissions and the risk of global climate change.

> Energy conservation: Because all natural materials are used, the amount of energy needed to operate an organic farm may be less than that required for the operation of a conventional farm.

> Improved animal health: Again, because synthetic chemicals are not introduced into the farming environment, animals living in the area of a farm may be at less risk to their own health and they may tend to live longer in the more healthful environment.

> Improved nutritional value: The use of only natural products in organic farming also tends to improve the health and nutritional value of crops that are grown and animals that are raised in such environments.

The evidence for these claims varies widely from relatively strong to virtually nonexistent. According to the report, for example, the impact of organic farming on soil quality as been "researched extensively," but, by contrast, there are "no quantitative data available" on climate change effects. The study does cite two other major European reports (similar reports from the United States are much less common) offering at least some support for the supposed environmental benefits of organic farming. For example, a report issued in January 2002 by the International Federation of Organic Agricultural Movements concluded that "there is a positive relationship between organic production and biodiversity conservation."

A report issued by the House of Lords European Communities Committee in 1999 reached a similar conclusion:

From the evidence that we have received, the claims for certain benefits of organic farming appear to be valid. This would be so for biodiversity, soil structure, water quality, most aspects of animal health and welfare, and some aspects of food quality.

Proponents of organic foods suggest that such foods have a number of benefits. They are convinced that such foods are more aesthetically pleasing, safer to eat, more nutritious, and better for the environment than are conventional foods. They often use arguments based on common sense or anecdotal evidence. Those claims may or may not be supported by scientific evidence. Such evidence now appears to suggest that the difference between organic and conventional foods may not be as profound or convincing as proponents of organic foods have argued in the past. Food sales data suggest that many people are convinced of the superiority of organic foods and are willing to pay a price premium to buy such foods.

## Criticisms of Organic Foods and Farming Techniques

As with other benefits claimed for organic farming and organic foods, research does not yet provide a clear and compelling case for the superiority of such procedures and products over conventional foods and farming techniques. Indeed, some scientists and laypersons take quite the opposite view. They go beyond simply denying the supposed benefits of organic foods and organic farming methods and suggest that such foods and practices may actually have harmful impacts on human health and the environment. This approach appears to reflect individuals' personal beliefs about organic foods, rather than a reasoned conclusion arising out of a study of scientific research, however. That is, there are zealots who simply feel strongly about the dangers or the "absurdity" of organic foods, just as there are fanatics who are totally committed to the promotion of such foods.

For example, freelance health and medical writer Marilynn Larkin wrote a 1991 column for the American Council on Science and Health's magazine *Priorities* on the "feeding frenzy" over organic foods. She claimed to be "horrified to discover that a new generation of activists seemed to have absorbed the same myths that she had adopted in the 1960s about the benefit of things 'organic.'" Larkin was concerned that the organic food movement was using "scare tactics and pseudoscience" to frighten the general public into believing that conventional foods are unsafe. She also objected to the use of federal money to support research on organic foods and to create and operate a program within the U.S. Department of Agriculture to certify organic foods. She argued that the program might prove to be so expensive that it would raise the cost of organic foods so much as to actually drive organic farmers out of business.

Although a few enthusiasts on both sides of the organic food issue overstate their cases, there are some reasons that a person might objectively question the safety of such foods and the methods by which they are produced. Probably the most commonly expressed concern relates to the possible existence of disease-causing microorganisms in organic foods, such as *E. coli 0157:H7*. As noted in chapter 5, illnesses caused by *E. coli 0157:H7* are among the most common food-borne diseases in the United States and other parts of the world. The use of pesticides on conventional crops limits to a significant extent the possibility that such bacteria will survive on those crops. Since organic farmers eschew the use of pesticides, however, that form of protection against food-borne illnesses is lost. The problem is compounded by the fact that one of the most common forms of fertilizer used by organic farmers is cow manure, a primary reservoir for the *E. coli 0157:H7* bacterium.

Critics of organic farming also question the importance organic consumers attribute to the absence of pesticides in organic foods. Conventional foods are already very carefully protected by laws and regulations that limit the amount of pesticide residue that is allowed on all kinds of foods, the skeptics say. Americans are not at risk from pesticide residues in the food, so, according to these critics, paying a premium price for organic foods does not make any sense.

Questions have been raised also about the supposed environmental benefits of organic farming. Some of the techniques used by organic farmers, such as extensive tillage, effectively loosen soil, promoting the growth and development of plants. However, some soil scientists suggest that such practices may actually reduce the mineral content of soil and lead to increased erosion.

As with so many topics in the field of food science, consumers are being presented with an increasing number of choices as to the kinds of foods available for purchase. A number and variety of legitimate arguments can be made for and against the use of organic farming techniques and the sale of organic foods. In most cases, convincing scientific evidence to support either side in these disputes is still lacking.

# Conclusion

Have humans come full circle with regard to their diet? At one time, many centuries ago, most peoples' diets were very simple. They ate the foods they grew themselves or that were available from nearby farms and dairies. The most complicated alimentary problems they faced often involved the development of methods to preserve food for seasons of the year when it was not immediately available.

That way of life persisted well into the 20th century, until the rise of modern chemistry during the century's early decades made possible a new and dramatically different way of looking at foods. Food scientists developed methods for transforming natural foods, not only to make them last longer, but also to make them more interesting and appealing to eat.

One of the first contributions of food chemistry was the invention and introduction of new types of food additives, chemicals that were capable of extending the shelf life of natural foods as well as increasing their aesthetic appeal. The use of food additives was hardly a new phenomenon in the 20th century, of course, but the additives developed by food chemists were the result of careful testing and development with some degree of assurance that the additives used would really contribute to an increase in the quality of foods to which they were added.

The introduction of a scientific approach to the development of food additives came at a time when public indignation had begun to demand closer control over the public food supply by the federal government. The Pure Food and Drug Act of 1906 was only the first of many efforts in the United States to ensure that alterations made in natural food were safe for humans and, to some extent, that they actually achieved some of the health and nutritional claims made for them. As food chemists extended the range of their research late in the 20th century to produce foods that differed very significantly from their natural state—and, in many case, produced entirely new and synthetic food products—governmental agencies have continued to be involved in efforts to make sure that such foods are safe and efficacious, efforts that have had mixed results.

By the last quarter of the 20th century, researchers had begun to take advantage of the full range of new materials and techniques that had been introduced into the field of chemistry to produce a virtually endless variety of new foods for consumers. In the most dramatic cases, entirely new food products were invented by introducing genes from one organism into another organism, the latter intended as a food for human consumption. Public reaction to such techniques varied widely, from enthusiastic acceptance to resistance that sometimes has bordered on the violent. In spite of the many studies that have been done so far, it is still not clear whether genetically modified foods pose any level of risk for human health or the natural environment or whether they will become yet one more ingenious addition to the arsenal of foods available to the modern consumer.

Interestingly enough, the reaction of some of those most concerned about genetically modified foods, food additives, the irradiation of foods, synthetic foods, and other products of research in modern food chemistry has been to renounce all or most of those advances (if advances they really are) and go back to simpler days. In early 2004, for example, the *New York Times Magazine* carried a feature story about a young man in Vermont who had opened an organic restaurant in which he served only those foods that he could obtain—insofar as possible—from farms, dairies, and other producers in the immediate area. Anyone reading that story might be excused for imagining that it could just as easily have been written a century ago, when the kinds of food that most people ate were precisely like those currently available in the "new" Vermont "farm-fresh" restaurant. Prices in the restaurant were significantly higher than those in more traditional restaurants that relied to a large extent on processed foods. But customers of the restaurant appeared not to be concerned about that fact and were willing to pay more to be able to buy fresh, whole, natural, organic foods, free of chemical treatment. Perhaps the most interesting point about the article was the response it drew from readers from around the country who praised the idea and looked forward to the day when a similar restaurant would be available in their area. As the author of the original story pointed out, there may perhaps be a market for a chain of similar restaurants that would bring to consumers a diet that many had thought had long passed them by.

So what is the future of the food industry in the United States and other developed nations of the world? Are we seeing just the beginning of a new age in foods, with an ever-increasing number and variety of synthetic or altered foods that we can hardly imagine today? Or are public concerns about health issues and possible risks to the environment of sufficient concern to cause governmental agencies to rein in the kinds of changes that researchers can make in foods and that food companies can offer to the public? Only the bravest souls will attempt to answer that question!

# GLOSSARY

**active packaging system (APS)**   A system of food preservation in which foods are sealed in a container that releases food additives that reduce spoilage of the food it contains.

**antisense insertion**   A process by which a DNA sequence is inserted into a host cell in reverse sequence.

**artificial sweetener**   A sweet-tasting synthetic food product that contains few or no calories.

**bioballistics**   A method for inserting genes into a host cell, in which thin metal slivers are coated with genes and fired into the cell by some mechanism, such as a gene gun; also called biolistics.

**browning**   The process that occurs when the surface of fruits, vegetables, and shellfish have been cut or bruised.

**Bt (or bt)**   An abbreviation for *Bacillus thuringiensis,* a soil bacterium that is highly toxic to a number of insects.

**calorie**   A unit of measurement of energy. A calorie is defined as the amount of heat energy needed to raise the temperature of 1 g of water by 1 °C. In nutrition, the term commonly refers to a kilocalorie, represented by an upper case *C* and correctly written as Calorie.

**chemical poration**   A method used to insert genes into host cells, in which cells are treated with some chemical to produce tiny openings in the cell walls. The pores allow genes to be inserted into the cell body more easily.

**chimera**   An organism that contains DNA from two or more different species.

**correction**   An action taken by a food company when food labels do not accurately reflect contents. Retailers make requested changes to food labels without returning products to the food-processing facility. Corrections do not involve foods that are unfit for human consumption.

**cross-contamination**   The transfer of pathogens from one food to another, either directly or indirectly.

**edible vaccine**   A vaccine that is produced when one or more genes for an antigen are added to some natural food.

**electroporation**   A method for inserting genes into host cells, in which cells are treated with an electrical shock to produce tiny pores in their cell walls, making it easier to insert genes into the cell body.

**enriched flour**   Flour (such as wheat flour) to which vitamins and minerals have been added to increase its nutritional value.

**enzyme**   A protein that catalyzes a biochemical reaction.

**ester**   A member of an organic family of compounds produced by the reaction between an organic acid and an alcohol.

**food danger zone**   That range of temperatures within which pathogens survive and reproduce most efficiently, between about 40 °F (4 °C) and 140 °F (60 °C).

**food infection**   A form of illness caused when bacteria and other microorganisms invade the digestive tract and colonize the intestinal epithelium.

**food intoxication**   A form of illness caused when bacteria release toxins into foods.

**food irradiation**   *See* IRRADIATION OF FOOD.

**food poisoning**   *See* FOOD INTOXICATION.

**food recall**   *See* RECALL.

**fortification**   The process of adding vitamins and minerals to foods that otherwise do not contain them or to foods that normally do contain them in higher concentrations.

**free radical**   An atom or molecule that contains at least one unpaired electron.

**gene gun**   A device for inserting DNA into a host cell.

**genetically engineered food**   *See* GENETICALLY MODIFIED FOOD.

**genetically modified food (GM food)**   Foods and food ingredients consisting of or containing genetically modified organisms, or produced from such organisms.

**health food**   A somewhat ambiguous term for any food that contributes to an overall improvement in a person's health.

**hydrogen bond**   A force of attraction between two polar molecules or two polar regions of unlike electrical charge.

**insecticidal crystal proteins (ICP)**   Proteins that are toxic to a wide variety of insects.

**irradiation of food**   A method of preserving food by treating it with X-rays, gamma rays, or some other form of high-energy radiation.

**laser poration**   A method for inserting genes into host cells, in which cells are exposed to a beam of laser light that produces tiny pores in their cell walls, making it easier to insert genes into the cell body.

**ligase**   An enzyme that catalyzes the formation of hydrogen bonds between two DNA fragments.

**lipid**   A member of an organic family of compounds characterized by its tendency to dissolve in alcohol, ether, chloroform, or other organic solvents, but not in water.

**market withdrawal**   An action taken by a food company in which a particular food product is no longer made available to retailers, for any number of reasons.

**microbial antagonists**   Organic and inorganic acids that retard or prevent spoilage by lowering the pH of food or by interrupting some essential biochemical reactions in a microbe.

**modified atmospheric packaging (MAP)**   A system of food preservation in which foods are sealed in a bag or other container from which oxygen has been removed.

**natural food**   A somewhat ambiguous term for foods that are minimally processed and free of artificial color, flavors, preservatives, and additives.

**organic food**   A somewhat ambiguous term defined by the U.S. government in the Organic Foods Protection Act of 1990 as any food produced by farmers who emphasize the use of renewable resources and the conservation of soil and water to enhance environmental quality for future generations.

**pH**   A measure of the acidity of an aqueous solution defined as the negative logarithm of the hydrogen ion concentration, or pH $= -\log[H^+]$.

**phytotoxin**   Any of a number of plant-generated chemicals that are toxic to a wide variety of animals, including bacteria, fungi, insects, herbivores, and human beings.

**precautionary principle**   The philosophical concept that governing bodies may be justified in taking regulatory actions even in cases where some scientific uncertainty remains regarding the possible risks and consequences of a given practice.

**protease**   An enzyme that breaks peptide bonds that link amino acids together in protein molecules.

**radiolysis**   The breaking of chemical bonds by radiation of any type.

**radiolytic products**   Fragments of molecules produced by the process of radiolysis.

**rancidity**   The process by which a fat or oil decomposes into its fundamental components, fatty acids and glycerol.

**recall**   An act taken by a food company when one of its products is found to be unsuitable for human consumption. Under a recall, foods are returned from a retailer to the food-processing company.

**recombinant DNA (rDNA) technology**   Any procedure by which DNA segments from two or more different species are combined to make a hybrid form of DNA.

**restriction endonuclease**   *See* RESTRICTION ENZYME.

**restriction enzyme**   An enzyme that recognizes specific base segments in a DNA molecule and then cuts those segments at specific positions.

**stock recovery**   An action taken by a food company in which the company has retailers return food products to it even though there may be nothing wrong with those foods.

**structured lipid (SL)**   Any lipid in which the position and character of fatty acid remnants in a lipid molecule have been altered from those found in the molecule's natural state.

**sulfite**   Any of a group of chemical species that includes sulfur dioxide ($SO_2$), sulfurous acid ($H_2SO_3$), the sulfite ion ($SO_3^{2-}$), and the bisulfite ion ($HSO_3^-$).

**traceability tag**   A piece of DNA added to genetically modified foods that has no effect on human health, the environment, or the organism into which it is inserted, but that provides an "address" of the company that made the product.

**transgenic organism**   *See* CHIMERA.

**unsaturation**   In organic chemistry, the presence of double or triple bonds in a compound.

**whole food**   A somewhat ambiguous term for any food that is as close to its whole and natural state as possible.

# FURTHER READING

## PRINT RESOURCES

Balkin, Karen. *Food-Borne Illnesses.* Farmington Hills, Mich.: Greenhaven Press, 2004.

Belitz, H. D., W. Grosch, and Peter Schieberle. *Food Chemistry.* New York: Springer Verlag, 2004.

Branen, Alfred Larry, P. Michael Davidson, Seppo Salminen, and John H. Thorngate III. *Food Additives: Revised and Expanded.* New York: Marcel Dekker, 2001.

Cliver, Dean, and Hans Riemann. *Foodborne Diseases.* 2nd edition. Philadelphia: Academic Press, 2002.

Dmitri, Carolyn, and Catherine Greene. "Recent Growth Patterns in the U.S. Organic Foods Market." ERS Agriculture Information Bulletin No. AIB777, September 2002. Washington, D.C.: Department of Agriculture, Economic Research Service. Also available online. URL: http://www. ers.usda.gov/publications/aib777/.

Francis, Frederick J., ed. *Wiley Encyclopedia of Food Science and Technology,* 2nd edition (4 vols.). New York: Wiley Interscience, 1999.

*Genetically Modified Foods: Experts View Regimen of Safety Tests as Adequate, but FDA's Evaluation Process Could Be Enhanced.* Washington, D.C.: General Accounting Office, Report GAO-02-566, May 2002. Also available online. URL: http://www.gao.gov/new.items/d02566.pdf.

Harris, Nancy. *Genetically Engineered Foods.* Farmington Hills, Mich.: Greenhaven Press, 2004.

Hui, Y. H., David Kitts, and Peggy S. Stanfield, eds. *Foodborne Disease Handbook.* New York: Marcel Dekker, 2001.

Janssen, Wallace F. "The Story of the Laws behind the Labels," *FDA Consumer,* June 1981. Also available online. URL: http://vm.cfsan.fda. gov/~lrd/history1.html.

Kramer, Klaus, Peter-Paul Hoppe, and Lester Packer. *Nutraceuticals in Health and Disease Prevention.* New York: Marcel Dekker, 2001.

Labbé, Ronald G., and Santos García, eds. *Guide to Foodborne Pathogens.* New York: John Wiley & Sons, 2001.

Loaharanu, Paisan, *Irradiated Foods,* 5th edition. New York: American Council on Science and Health, 2003. Also available online. URL: http://www.acsh.org/publications/pub/D.198/pub_detail.asp.

*Low Calorie Sweeteners and Health.* Washington, D.C.: International Food Information Council Foundation, October 2001. Also available online. URL: http://www.ific.org/publications/reviews/sweetenerir.cfm.

Molins, R. A., ed. *Food Irradiation: Principles and Applications.* New York: Wiley Interscience, 2001.

Nestle, Marion. *Food Politics.* Berkeley: University of California Press, 2002.

Nottingham, Stephen. *Eat Your Genes: How Genetically Modified Food Is Entering Our Diet* (Revised and Updated Edition). London: Zed Books, 2003.

"Organic Foods," Series of articles from *Consumer Reports,* various dates. Citations available online. URL: http://www.consumersunion.org/i/ Food_Safety/Organic_Foods.

Rowell, Andrew. *Don't Worry, It's Safe to Eat: The True Story of GM Food, BSE, & Foot and Mouth.* London: Earthscan Publications, 2003.

Saltmarch, Michael, and Judy Buttriss, eds. *Functional Foods II: Claims and Evidence.* London: Royal Society of Chemistry, 2000.

Schlosser, Eric. *Fast Food Nation: The Dark Side of the All-American Meal.* New York: Houghton Mifflin, 2001.

Watson, David, ed. *Food Chemical Safety: Additives. Vol. II.* Boca Raton, Fla.: CRC Press, 2002.

Watson, Ronald R., ed. *Functional Foods & Nutraceuticals in Cancer Prevention.* Ames: Iowa State University, 2003.

Winter, Ruth. *A Consumer's Dictionary of Food Additives.* New York: Three Rivers Press, 1999.

## INTERNET RESOURCES

Center for Food Safety and Applied Nutrition. "Everything Added to Food in the United States." Center for Food Safety and Applied Nutrition, U.S. Food and Drug Administration. Available online. URL: http://www. cfsan.fda.gov/~dms/eafus.html. Page generated October 23, 2006.

———. "Food Ingredients and Packaging: Consumer Information." U.S. Food and Drug Administration, Center for Food Safety and Applied Nutrition. Available online. URL: http://www.cfsan.fda.gov/~dms/opa-bckg.html. Downloaded September 17, 2006.

Center for Science in the Public Interest. "CPSI's Guide to Food Additives." Center for Science in the Public Interest. Available online. URL: http:// www.cspinet.org/reports/chemcuisine.htm. Downloaded September 17, 2006.

Code of Federal Regulations, Chapter 21, Parts 73 and 74. Available online. URL: http://www.access.gpo.gov/nara/cfr/waisidx_06/21cfr73_06.html and http://www.access.gpo.gov/nara/cfr/waisidx_06/21cfr74_06.html. A list of approved food additives for coloring.

———. Chapter 21, Part 181. Available online. URL: http://www.access.gpo. gov/nara/cfr/waisidx_06/21cfr181_06.html. A list of prior-sanctioned food additives.

———. Parts 182 and 184. Available online. URL: http://www.access.gpo. gov/nara/cfr/waisidx_06/21cfr182_06.html and http://www.access.gpo. gov/nara/cfr/waisidx_06/21cfr184_06.html. A list of GRAS food additives.

Cornell Cooperative Extension. "Genetically Engineered Organisms." Public Issues Education Project. Available online. URL: http://www. geo-pie.cornell.edu/gmo.html. Downloaded September 17, 2006.

Donaldson, Liam, and Sir Robert May, "Health Implications of Genetically Modified Foods," U.K. Department of Health, May 1999. Available online. URL: http://www.dh.gov.uk/assetRoot/04/06/50/90/04065090. pdf. Downloaded September 17, 2006.

Genomics.energy.com. "Genetically Modified Foods and Organisms." Human Genome Project. Available online. URL: http://www.ornl.gov/ sci/techresources/Human_Genome/elsi/gmfood.shtml. Downloaded September 17, 2006.

How Stuff Works. "What Are Genetically Modified (GM) Foods?" Available online. URL: http://home.howstuffworks.com/question148.htm. Downloaded September 17, 2006.

Jacobson, Michael F. "Liquid Candy: How Soft Drinks Are Harming Americans' Health." Center for Science in the Public Interest. Available online. URL: http://www.cspinet.org/new/pdf/liquid_candy_final_w_ new_supplement.pdf. Downloaded September 17, 2006.

The Mellman Group. "Recent Poll Findings." Available online. URL: http:// pewtrusts.org/pdf/biotech_poll_091803.pdf. Downloaded September 17, 2006.

National Agricultural Statistics Service. Prospective Plantings. National Agricultural Statistics Service. Available online. URL: http://usda. mannlib.cornell.edu/usda/current/ProsPlan/ProsPlan-03-31-2006.pdf. Downloaded January 15, 2007.

Organic Consumers Association. "Organics: OCA's Resource Center on Organic Farming, Organic Labeling, and Organic Standards." Available online. URL: http://www.organicconsumers.org/organlink.htm. Downloaded September 17, 2006.

Pusztai, Arpad. "Genetically Modified Foods: Are They a Risk to Human/ Animal Health?" Available online. URL: http://www.actionbioscience. org/biotech/pusztai.html. Downloaded September 17, 2006.

Union of Concerned Scientists. "Food and Environment," Available online. URL: http://www.ucsusa.org/food_and_environment/index.cfm. Downloaded September 17, 2006.

Wylie-Rosett, Judith. "Fat Substitutes and Health." American Heart Association Health Statement. Available online. URL: http://circ. ahajournals.org/cgi/content/full/105/23/2800#TBL1. Originally published in the AHA journal *Circulation,* 105:2800, 2002.

# INDEX